what do you believe?

What Do You Believe?

Derek Beres, editor

Outside the Box Publishing
Brooklyn

Outside the Box Publishing
323 3rd St #8
Brooklyn NY 11215
www.otbpublishing.com

Cover design by Jeff Gamble
www.jeffgamble.com

Warrior design by Craig Anthony Miller
www.craiganthonymiller.com

Interior Design by Derek Beres

ISBN-13: 978-0-9817398-7-8
ISBN-10: 0-9817398-7-3

The Nature of Belief

One evening after an especially lively night of basketball in Jersey City—our Monday night ritual for some years—Dax and I were discussing the nature of belief. I had just read a survey or poll or something of the like discussing Christianity and atheism and science, and I proposed the idea of an anthology about this topic. Dax mulled it over a minute. We stopped on Wayne St, a bitter cold winter wind whipping up the block, and he said no, that's too complex; something simpler would be more appropriate, something fundamental to the question of belief. Adding science and godlessness and all those things would be distracting, subjecting the essayists to slants. We wanted something less angular, more straight forward. Hence the seemingly simple and yet rather complex question: What do you believe?

We decided to put forth those four words to our friends and see what came in. By being ambiguous—sometimes we were asked "Believe in what?," to which our reply was: Exactly—we hoped to push forward the dialogue. And so it goes with this collection now in your hands. We did not limit the question to "writers," i.e. people who actively write for a profession. Of course, some of these essays are written by pros; however, not all. Like myself, I'm betting you'll be hard put to guess which of these essayists write "professionally," as they are all excellent contributions.

They are not excellent because of their styles, per se, but because of their content, and most of all, their honesty. Over and again, I received emails stating that the question seemed so easy when first heard, yet when the person sat down to type what it was they believed, a giant blank screen confronted them viciously, laughing all the way. This is good—by challenges we grow. And it is often the case that not until your beliefs are challenged can you state with confidence what it is that you actually believe. "Blind" and "faith" are two of the dirtiest words I know when used together. Not exploring your beliefs leads to dangerous assumptions.

But enough of that; I don't want to spoil a thing. The nature of this collection will be told through its writers, not by me telling you what to think. I sincerely thank every contributor inside of these pages for making manifest this idea, for their time and effort in living up to the challenge. And I hope that you, the reader, will be equally challenged and inspired while flipping through these pages, and have as much fun as I did along the way.

—Derek Beres
Brooklyn, NY, April 2009

What Do You Believe?

Against My Will

Dax-Devlon Ross

Back in seventh grade, Wednesdays meant one thing: Meeting for Worship. At approximately 10:30, school would effectively shut down and, along with our "Teams" (i.e. homerooms), we'd file from the main building to the Old Gym, where for the next thirty-five minutes the entire middle school body sat in quiet contemplation. You weren't supposed to get up and use the bathroom, nor were you allowed to partake in any other such restless adolescent activities as talking, passing notes, passing out, or completing any errant homework assignments. This isn't to say none of this went on; certainly whenever a group of pre-teens and teens are gathered in a room for an extended period of time over a number of years their preternatural ingenuity occasionally outwits the vigilant oversight of their elders—but only occasionally. Generally speaking, we knew all too well that there were eyes secretly ascertaining our slightest gestures, and that a summons to Principal Williams's office could be awaiting us upon return to the school building.

Frankly, I hated Meeting for Worship. To a pubescent body there is little worse than being told to sit still in a gym, of all places, and for a half-hour no less. Granted, you could talk, that is if you were willing to stand up in front of the whole school and share some deep and personal note of familial pain, worldly woe, or spiritual yearning. Meeting for Worship, I was told upon entering the Sidwell Friends School as one of five new black students accepted that year—the only one in my section— was one of the unique features that set it apart from other preparatory schools in the Washington, D.C. area. Other such discerning qualities (ones I can remember at least) were 1) the five-minute moment of silence we observed at the beginning of each day and before lunch, 2) calling our ex-hippie/tree-hugger teachers by their first names, and 3) receiving ungraded progress reports instead of letter grades each marking period. Coming from a mostly black public school, Meeting for Worship was, to paraphrase one of my present students, "some corny white people nonsense." Just about the only thing I looked forward to on Wednesday mornings was the Meeting for Learning that followed Meeting for Worship. This was the non-compulsory part of the Wednesday morning ritual. You could, at your leisure and if you felt so inclined, drop by the Meeting for Learning room to chat with others about some of the issues raised in that day's Meeting for Worship. Clearly, at twelve, this wasn't my intent. At thirty, I'd like to say I was concerned with world affairs of the day, but my motives for attending were far less noble—all of the O.J. and cream cheese bagels you could handle. And since I usually came to school hungry (due to no fault of my parents mind you), I was often the first person in line for a cinnamon raisin bagel, after which, O.J. in tow, I dipped out of the door before the meeting officially began, and made for the staircase.

Meeting for Worship wasn't my only middle school nemesis. There were plenty of utterly dull activities I was forced to endure. I'll spare you by sticking with the ones that left the most lasting impact. At the beginning of each school year, each "Team" went on a four-day camping trip. All of the other Teams routinely shoved off to sites that had ready-built cabins and mess halls, but not Team III, which was the team to which I was assigned during my first day of school. Team III had all of the 'crunchy' pedagogues. They wore Birkenstocks, faded dungarees, plaid, tie-dye, sundresses, and face glasses. Had I known better at the time, I would've pronounced them Deadheads from the start. They were great and passionate teachers, patient with my unmotivated ass to no end, but they were also the most radical, so when it came time for camping trips, we had to rough it. We slept in tents; we each were given KP duty; we had required day hikes and campfire sing-alongs—the whole corny nine yards. I hated every second of it, and when a thunderstorm swept through our campsite and literally lifted 95% of the tents out of the ground on the last night of our stay, I watched my fellow students sprint for cover from inside my remarkably stable tent, gleefully thinking, "Ha! That oughta teach them to make us sleep in tents!" Needless to say, I awoke with a strange infection in my eyes that required me to walk around my neighborhood looking like I'd just caught a two-piece from "Iron" Mike Tyson (not to be mistaken for the chump who sometimes fights under the same name). It was my first true lesson in karma being a bitch.

Then there was the four-day rock climbing expedition my art teacher and mentor Rick signed me up for, even after I explained that it was better for all concerned parties if I just took the four days off and come back on Monday. Months earlier I'd been given a list of activities I could choose to participate in for mini-mester, a sort of annual career exploration week. But since I didn't see anything having remotely to do with being a professional basketball player, I chose the path of least resistance, only to receive a call at home that Monday morning (I had artfully explained to my mother that we had the option of participating or staying home for the week) indicating that I needed to be at school ASAP. Having missed the sign-up dates for every other even remotely interesting activity, I was forcibly enlisted in the granola group, handed a brown bag lunch, and driven out to various rock climbing locations for a week, where I watched my crunchy classmates climb themselves silly. After a singularly embarrassing slip, whereupon my Air Jordans (the Threes in case you were wondering: black with red trim, one of the illest versions on record) were fatally scratched, I solemnly refused to participate in any rock climbing, and instead wandered through the woods with my secretly stashed *Straight Outta Compton* tape blasting through my Walkman. In retrospect, I was afraid, very afraid of trying something I wasn't already good at in front of people whom I already believed doubted my abilities. Such was the plight of the black kid in the white school. Let's move on.

Community Service: hated it! Again, an overnight 'experience' we were required to participate in. In this case Sidwell decided it was a good idea to donate its students' services to every soup kitchen, meals on wheels van, and homeless shelter in the city. From what I recall, Community Service took place twice a year, as did the camping trips. We'd have to bring a sleeping bag and a change of clothes to school one day, and right after school we'd take a bus over to Mt. Pleasant, where after being briefed by our community service liaison we commenced to hand out dinners. I didn't quite understand why we needed to be there, seeing as they were clearly capable of handing out dinners from the back of the vans with the staff they already had, but there we were anyway, passing out brown bag dinners, dinners, if I remember correctly, we also ate. After our work was done, we'd head to a homeless shelter and feed more people before retiring to a church in Georgetown that offered us their creaky pews as beds for the night. By five o'clock we were back up and, after washing up, loading onto the cheesebox that was waiting to chug us to our early morning destination: a soup kitchen. We set tables, mopped floors, prepared plates. And when the homeless began arriving for breakfast, we were there to greet them. After breakfast, we had to clean up the dining hall before heading to our final destination, a battered women's shelter. There we spent the afternoon helping to care for small children. I can still remember counting the minutes before the whole ordeal was over. I couldn't wait to get back on the bus and go back to our side of town, and open my refrigerator and sleep in my own bed and forget all about the homelessness problem.

I wound up staying at Sidwell for six years and ultimately graduating, though I can hardly say I did so with much of an appreciation for Meeting for Worship or any of the other values the school tried to instill in me. When I left, like most eighteen year-olds, I was just glad to be gone, through with that place that I had come to associate with bondage. When a year later I was suddenly popping out passionately argued poli-sci papers in favor of Communism (one of which a professor actually called me aside for and warned me about before showing me the "A-" he'd given me), I never stopped to think back to Sidwell. When two years later I decided to study Philosophy and English Literature because they seemed like the degrees a black male was least likely to pursue, it never registered that perhaps the hours of quiet contemplation that Sidwell had provided me with had somehow prepared me to challenge the status quo in my own ways. When four years later I was firing off enraged editorials in the school paper and filling private journals with melancholic musings, it never much dawned on me that perhaps in six years of compulsory silence I had developed reliance upon deep inner reflection. When I grew out my hair and took up hiking as my hobby of choice, I never thought back to those four-day hiatuses into the wild I had to be dragged to for two years of middle school. When at twenty-six I came to what I felt was an honest and heartfelt conclusion that practicing law was not something I could do in good conscience, I didn't credit Sidwell for instilling in me high, if not idealistic, ethical notions. And when I finally gravitated toward education, I didn't do so because of my teachers at Sidwell who'd said that I should share my time, talents, and gifts.

Like a lot of Christians-by-default in this country, I grew up without any rigorous religious rituals. Although I was sent to Sunday school for a number of years, my family didn't go to church. Looking at it now, I believe my being sent was more of a political move on the part of my mother. Ours was a chatty, tight-knit community, and after the divorce she didn't want people to think badly of the family. I despised Sunday school. It was full of banalities, none of which I can muster the willpower or wherewithal to remember. Then at a certain point my buddy G.G. and I realized that we could spend our offering money on an Egg McMuffin at McDonald's and still make it to church in time for O.J. and cookies without being struck down en route. After a while, rather than even bother stopping in for refreshments, we decided to try our luck and walk our polyester suit wearing behinds right on by Northminster Presbyterian. Together we planned to sleep through the alarm the following Sunday just to see what our parents would do; sure enough no one bothered to wake us. I'm almost positive a few uneasy phone conversations were shared between our parents, but seeing as they were ostensible heathens themselves, there was hardly much they could do or say to us without appearing more hypocritical to our emerging awareness of the contradictory adult world swirling around us. From then on the only times I stepped foot in the sterile Northminster basement was for my cub scout meetings, which after a minor scandal involving the suspicious completion of my entire cub scout task book in record time, I vowed never to attend again.

Sidwell was my dad's idea. He understood better than I did that there was so much he just didn't have the time to share with me, but that he wanted me to experience. He was the one who arranged the interviews; the one who came by the house early in the morning and drove me to Carroll, where I sat in a cold Catholic school cafeteria taking a test all day long; the one who called my mother's house and told me I'd gotten in; the one who shelled out thousands every year just to keep me in, even during the recession, when his business was bankrupt. I would often offer him the option of sending me to a less expensive school, even to a public high school, but he wouldn't even pay attention to me. Even after Billy the-wayward-lacrosse-coach Dean called me out of class one day to inform me that I couldn't return to school until the bill was paid, daddy-o came through in the clutch better than any Sunday afternoon playmaker.

Aside from the campus cult that my roommate endeavored to initiate me in during our sophomore year, I can't recall stepping foot in a house of worship during my time at Rutgers. I do, however, vaguely recall stopping in front of a church while driving, reciting a quiet prayer the day my girlfriend threatened to dump me if I didn't stop smoking pot, but since I never actually stepped foot inside that church, I can't officially count that. By then I had been thoroughly indoctrinated in a secular lifestyle complete with rationalizations, defenses, and various other means of denying the spirit within that I believed I didn't need to believe anything. The most useful of my obfuscations became philosophy. Philosophy was the collegiate pseudo-intellectual's weapon of choice. It endowed you with the unprecedented power to simply not give a fuck, but to do so backed by plausible theory. You could a) logically disprove the existence of a higher power or b) metaphysically absolve the necessity of a God that "created" existence. It was quite a rush. Once I was introduced to the writing of Sartre and Camus, it was over. My cursory understanding of existentialism led me to disavow all ethical responsibilities, to bask in the irreverent glow of despair. By the time I entered my Marxian "religion is the opiate of the masses" stage, the only remaining belief I had was in the ultimate and irretrievable depravity of modern civilization. Take away the thin veil of political hostility, and I was little more than twenty-something grump.

Luckily shallow political arrogance such as mine becomes difficult to sustain in the face of day-to-day survival, and on a Sunday at the tail end of a nine-month unemployment stint back in '03, I found myself in the bathroom mirror wondering where it all went wrong. Over the previous two years, my relatively mild mood swings had grown into drawn-out depressions that I artfully hid from everyone except the one closest to me, who of course bore the brunt of my inner turmoil. The gist of my anguish was this: I was lost. There was no crisis I was trying to stem, no addiction I was trying to shake, no love I needed to get over, no loss I was trying to confront. I was just lost.

Enter Buddhism. A mere week after my morning of reckoning, I was sitting in a SGI meeting chanting excerpts from the Lotus Sutra to a Gohonzon. It felt good. It felt right. And for the next year I earnestly pursued my faith with an open mind and a pure heart. A month after my first meeting, I was conferred my own Gohonzon at the SGI cultural center in Manhattan, after which sponsoring members visited me to help me establish a proper practice domain in my apartment. With my prayer beads, my incense and bell, I began chanting in earnest twice a day. I went to weekly meetings and began volunteering weekends at the cultural center. SGI became a part of my life on every level. When I was having rough moments, I turned to the Gohonzon. When I had spiritual questions, I turned to the Gosho, or to the writings of President Daisaku Ikeda. I became versed in SGI-speak and began talking about my "determinations," my efforts toward "world peace," my "human revolution," "gratitude," and other phrases. It was refreshing to be among a group of people who refused to take a defeatist attitude, and inspiring to see the strides many members were making in their lives. Even when I began to wonder why our study of the Lotus Sutra and other integral texts was so limited; even when I found myself mouthing mantras that felt more suitable for pep-rallies or Tony Robbins seminars; even when I started getting phone calls from members I had never met before who wanted to talk about how I could "further my practice"—even after all of that, I continued to aspire to live by SGI Buddhism's fundamental beliefs: happiness of all people. It was of little concern at the time that "happiness" as a goal is both elusive and somewhat superficial. I believed I was happier. I was chanting hard twice a day, attending meetings, volunteering, taking on official posts ...

Then my dad got sick. When I reported this information to the other members, I was told to chant for him, and that they would do the same. Members would call to tell me they'd sent special chants for my father, and when he did go through a period of convalescence we were all too quick to lay the credit at the doorstep of our collective efforts. At that point my chanting became a near obsession. I became convinced that if I didn't chant for several hours a day, my dad's growth would swell up as punishment for my laxity. I didn't want to believe this, but I couldn't help it; it was beyond me. I had put so much faith into the power of the Gohonzon and the nam-myoho-renge-kyo that giving it up would mean regression, and in my father's case, death.

At my weakest point the phone calls really started. I was being asked how many people I spoken to about SGI and whether or not I was encouraging others (i.e. my friends and family) to join. Those who did bring in new members were being applauded and spoken about as if they were salesmen of the month. Those who weren't bringing in new members (like myself) were discretely chastised. Frankly, it got weird, and after one meeting too many, I got out. For a while I chanted on my own, but even that didn't sit right anymore. For one, I didn't even know the meaning of the words I was chanting! When I'd ask others they didn't know either. The message was clear enough: it wasn't about the meaning of the words, but about the outcomes they produced. So long as I was living the "winning life," nothing else mattered.

Maybe it was that simple. Maybe I didn't need to look deeper into it. Maybe my problem was too much philosophy and not enough faith. Either way, once I felt the pressure to bring in more members, I couldn't be a part of the practice anymore. I didn't and don't disparage SGI, but I felt the danger for slippage was too great. People believe what they are led to believe; they follow the path they are called to follow. Moreover, the pursuit of worldly success that the practice stressed lacked an ethical underpinning. While certain strains of Christianity preach tolerance, acceptance, piety, and suffering as a means of salvation, SGI took the opposite approach: religion as the individual's vehicle to happiness in whichever form said individual seeks it. There was no critical thought about what happiness is, nor a conversation about at whose expense one person's idea of happiness may come.

Cutting my losses didn't come without its share of guilt. There were many phone calls to avoid and awkward street encounters to expedite. I had to gently explain to members that I would no longer be attending meetings. After a few earnest weeks of chanting, my butsudan was removed and placed in the dusty corner of my room before meeting the curb one Sunday morning. Eventually, I rolled up the Gohonzon and put it out of view. That was almost two years ago.

In six years I only spoke at one Meeting for Worship—the last meeting of my senior year. After years of listening to other more courageous students stand and bear their souls, I decided to stand and share my thoughts on the Sidwell experience. By then I'd cut my share of Meetings, opting for an occasional haircut instead of the silence. One Wednesday I borrowed a buddy's car and spent the morning at a young lady's house, in her bed. But on this Wednesday it dawned on me that I'd never sit through Meeting for Worship as a Sidwell student again. Sentimentality kicked in and up I shot. I won't go so far as to conjure the content of my speech, because I'm sure it was nowhere near as heartfelt or poignant as the girl who once stood up during the dreadful '92 recession and announced that she was leaving the school since her father had lost his job. They had already put their house up for sale. This was to be her last Meeting for Worship. For fourteen years that student's words have echoed in my consciousness as perhaps the most courageous outpouring of raw emotion outside of a wedding or funeral that I've ever witnessed. I remember her crying and I remember her friends engulfing her when she sat back down. I remember my own sadness for a girl I merely passed in the halls, and I remember thinking how unfair it was that she had to leave a life she clearly loved due to no fault of her own.

Six years is a long time. Over the course of that many years, particularly adolescent years, you're shaped in ways that aren't readily apparent to you. Values get instilled that remain dormant until you're faced with an experience that calls them into action. That's been very much the case with my experiences at Sidwell. As much as I dreaded them at the time, every one of the lessons I was forced to endure—be they to appreciate nature, to value silence, to share your talents with others, to offer your time to the less fortunate—have all come to define who I aspire to be in life. This isn't to say I don't seek worldly success, but it is to say that I try not to commingle my pursuit of money with my pursuit of divinity. What I believe isn't so much the product of being force-fed religion as it is of being pushed and shoved along at a young enough age that it made a difference in who I was to become. I believe that if we want a better world, then we need to raise better people. We have to not only expose, but also impose the values we hold in the highest esteem onto children. They can't be given a choice about certain things, particularly those that a society relies upon for its sustenance, like community service, and the appreciation of nature, and the sharing of our time. It's not always enough to show a person the way to goodness. In some cases they need to be prodded along the path, even against their will.

www.daxdevlonross.com

Holding Empty

Jill Ettinger

There's a lot going on in this world, all the time. From the frozen corners to the deepest oceans, this Earth is alive. In a breathtaking moment, everything changes, when we realize that we are not living on top of the planet as separate, but as an intrinsic part of it, from start to finish. Like Miles Davis's classic jazz recording *Kind of Blue*, life is an inexplicable masterpiece with little instruction and lots of improvisation—a lot to consider when asked to write about what I believe. It's a question of my perception and experiences, and in earnest, spending almost thirty-five years in this being, I wouldn't say I know a whole heck of a lot more than I did the day I arrived. As I type these words though, anything can happen.

I started writing this essay at least half a dozen different times since being invited to do so more than a month ago. I kept getting the feeling like I was forcing something, so I resigned to let this much-anticipated December in New Jersey settle into me, and hopefully dislodge these words from wherever it is they've been stuck to. The most noticeable challenge in this task has been that I don't so much think of myself as a writer. I'm definitely not in the same league as the publishers of this book, both brilliant authors, nor am I probably as seasoned as some of the other contributors to this collective effort. Perhaps a more accurate description of my writing résumé would be along the lines of "randomly documented thinking." There is a gap between myself and the limitless possibilities of what to write about that I often sink into, rather than repel. I'm not saying this as cautionary, or to rally any sort of sympathy or pity from the reader. It's just the truth about how I view my relationship to the written word. Nonetheless, I've written for the better part of my life.

In my youth, I penned a lot of poems. I'm curious by nature, and poetry, so often abstract, fascinated me. Though I don't write poetry very often anymore, many of my views on the human condition were shaped through the poetry I read as a teenager. What little I remember about high school is not the curriculum that was forced on me, but the books I brought with me, like Rainer Maria Rilke's *Possibility of Being*, Charles Baudelaire's *Flowers of Evil*, Arthur Rimbaud's *A Season in Hell*, and the collected poems of Dylan Thomas and ee cummings. Over the last decade I've written a few articles and music reviews, but mostly scores of journal entries. I realized how easily we forget the details of our lives, mostly remembering only key events and moments, but I find the details hold a special place in my heart. Looking forward to looking back, I make an effort to record the details of my life.

I've also always longed to write with more discipline. Books fascinate me, from the good to the unbearably bad; both share the undeniable passion and discipline of a writer. At different points in my life, I've outlined concepts of books I plan

23

on writing someday, not getting much further along in the process than that. Oh, it's because I have a full-time job and a full-time life and I travel so much and yes, it's all just excuses, I'm well aware. But it is where I'm at, and though it's slightly frustrating, there's something in the irritation that I'm comfortable with, because it keeps reminding me of what it is I must do someday. Even if a lot farther away than right now, I know someday is bound to arrive before too long.

Part of my process as a writer-to-be includes a clandestine blue zipper canvas bag filled with, well, my thoughts. I got the bag five or six years ago while working for a company called Yogi Tea. It was a freebie give-away at a trade show promoting one of their top-sellers, also one of my favorites: Organic Green Tea with Kombucha. It's a healthy immune-supporting tonic with a fruity flavor and floral aroma. The box design is pictured on one side with the quote "Master the Art of Tea" subtly written underneath the image. I've always liked the quote because, unlike most blatant self-promoting efforts that mega-brands are known to do, this one doesn't read "Master of the Art of Tea." Instead, it invites self-discovery and exploration into what one might consider artistic about the ritual, rather than pontificating on about how this particular brand houses the real tea masters.

Housing my words was an unintentional use of the bag, but now I recognize a pleasant similarity between the tea it boasts on the outside and the writing hidden inside. Many beverages are often called tea, but the word actually only applies to one plant: Camellia Sinensis. Though various processes determine the type of tea it will eventually be known as (white undergoes no oxidization, green very slightly, oolong halfway, and black fully oxidized), they all start out the same leaf. Like the tea plant's numerous adulterations, writing originates from that floating, mysterious place of human inspiration, and finds itself transformed and individualized like a cup of tea, hopefully full of sweet sipping and mindful contemplating. If there is one tangible thing I believe in, that is most definitely: a perfect cup of tea.

Over the years and attempts at documenting this life I'm experiencing, I've accumulated a mass of journals and notebooks all used to capture the thought of the moment, and of course the ever-important after thoughts. There is a tattered fuzzy green journal I took on my first trip out of the country to Australia when I was twenty-one; the hard metal cased binder from my bicycle messenger days filled with scribbled on call tags, envelopes, and receipts; a blue spiral notebook from my yoga teacher training course and stacks of various other notebooks and pads. How these all ended up in this bag I'm not exactly sure. Most likely a coordinated effect of moving at one time or another, and then, realizing there wasn't yet a proper place to unpack these thoughts, this extension of myself just came to call this bag home. As my journals are filled each year, they too now meet their blue canvas fate. I use a computer of course, but writing is writing and there is a certain release in putting pen to paper that I'm sure I'll be fond of playing with for the rest of my life. So, I suppose one day, I'll outgrow the bag and move onto something larger.

Two or three times a year I bring the bag out of the closet and do the obligatory dumpster dive search and rescue. Thousands of starter thoughts rest in there, fodder for eventual books, I tell myself as I gaze upon this rather sloppy self-history hoping a story will startle me and leap out from a black-and-white speckled Mead composition notebook all perfectly typed and edited, ready for the publishers. That hasn't happened, yet.

I know a few people who feel so comfortable with their lives that they've completely transcended their past and burned all their journals. Shortly after high school, I tossed two notebooks that I had lived by. My relationship to those critical years now relies mainly on memories and shared stories, instead of tangible documentation. The desperate teenage angst that bled into morbid poetry and prose no longer had a purpose, or so I thought in my early twenties. It was an embarrassment. Burn it. At the time it was a cathartic process, but I've often speculated in the fifteen or so years since destroying those journals that if we cannot look at and understand what something is, how can we begin to learn from it, or let it go? Time opens up that space to be able to reflect, to reassess, to see something we missed. Mirrors are more than just the pieces of glass we surround ourselves with in forced obsessions with our physical circumstance. Mirrors are the experiences that have led us to our present condition. Sometimes a mirror is in a friend's soft eyes, and sometimes the quick, cold glare of a stranger. Who we are is a complex collage of reflections.

This essay project fueled one last glance into my bag of thoughts for the year, with the question "What DO I believe?" swirling around in my brain. It's a question I've asked myself many times, always with a different answer. Thinking back again to the vague direction Davis used to construct *Kind of Blue*, I thought, as I laid eyes on this journal entry from May18, 2004, everything is like jazz:

> We all must come full circle in our beliefs. Any practice, ritual, tradition; any commitment binds us, keeps us pursuing a discipline whose rigidity in reality serves only as that chosen path and nothing more. To keep from the abstract, it matters not then if we live our lives in pursuit of the highest possible vibration or that of one diving into the darkest realms. We can then lie, cheat, steal, murder, deep fry, just as easily as serve, love, give, purify, meditate. However it began no matter, it is our concepts of right and wrong, black and white, that carry into our consciousness the acceptance of concepts altogether. But the true reality, perhaps, actually rests in the abstract. Our predisposition to create order out of chaos seems to be our most noticeable disorder. We suffer from the delusion that ordering our existence somehow also unravels it. But to what model do we hold our work-in-progress up to? How can anything we profess or believe in ever be comparable to anything but itself?

Einstein said that time exists because otherwise everything would be happening all at once. Throughout the timeline, life transforms itself from the collection of experiences. Proof is in the pudding as the saying goes—value exists where we place it. Yet separating ourselves from all experiences is what it means to be truly present—to be in the "all-at-once," a daunting task even in our deepest meditations. That space where value has no value seems to be of greatest value after all. Perhaps what we believe matters not as much as what we do with it.

After my six-week tour of Australia, my fuzzy green journal and I returned to the states, me now a mature, world-traveling 22-year-old with a taste for Vegemite, the journal barely half full. It was not only a first trip to another country, but one to another world. It was a journey of incredible transformation. I had given up on college, traveled with the Grateful Dead, done more than my share of drugs, but Australia made me a believer of the unbelievable. In the presence of Tasmanian Devils, giant kangaroos, emus and duck-billed platypuses, the painted cliffs of Mariah Island, the "Twelve Apostles" limestone formation off the great ocean road, and a rare viewing of the southern lights, I wrote on Feb 14, 1994: "From the edge of the deep green forest … with each breath I take in the sights offered before me, and with each exhale I let go the millions of questions I am left to ponder of this excellent planet."

Sometimes, just seeing is believing.

To balance out all the post-Oz bong hits I was doing, and for lack of a better mode of transportation (I didn't even get a driver's license until I was 25—I was an avid cyclist), the trip down under had enhanced my sweet spot for the exhilarating. I needed a job, making me a prime candidate for the bicycle messenger culture of Pittsburgh.

An older city, Pittsburgh was married to the industrial revolution. Over 95 million tons of steel poured out of the area during World War II, making slag heaps out of its Golden Triangle's three rivers (the Allegheny, Ohio, and Monongahela;

yes, that's right, Monongahela—sound it out...). Up from collapsed mill valleys grew metal and glass spires of modernity, and a new city happily embraced the move into the technological era. While the smoke and soot subsided, the city became home to Fortune 500 companies like Alcoa, HJ Heinz, PNC, and United Steel. It is a town with a big heart and real, honest working-class people who take pride in their families and communities. A rich culture continues to thrive in the city's many ethnic neighborhoods, museums, and universities.

Environment dictates our relationship to it. I remember as a child that the abandoned steel mills looked to me like some sort of mutated alien spaceships. I thought they were ubiquitous, that every town had them. Their presence filled me with awe and fear. What on Earth went on inside those things? My parents told me they were abandoned mills, but I found it difficult to believe that something so big was empty. Why had they not been torn down, or turned into something else? Just one generation before, they were in full production, blazing out steel, fire, and smoke, but now their purpose was veiled to a curious child in search of consequence.

Rusting architecture aside, Pittsburgh is beautiful. I've been fortunate enough to visit many major cities across this country, and while I hold a special place in my heart for my hometown, it is with an objective eye that I tell you of its commanding view. The three rivers meet at a point, forming the Golden Triangle, which is said to be sitting atop valuable crystal mineral deposits. The way the city shoots up from that point actually conjures such images. Pittsburgh is home to more bridges than any other US city, including the Smithfield Street, the oldest and longest figure-eight bridge in the country, also my all-time favorite. It was bridges like this one, rather than buildings, that made me particularly impressed with man-made structures. Like buildings, their reliance and utility are critical, but no one sits at a desk on the top of a bridge. You get to the other side and keep on moving. As part of the environment I was exposed to all my life, I had come to assume bridges were nothing special. But once I became an intimate traveler of the dozens of bridges, unique to Pittsburgh, a deeper understanding and appreciation would turn to profound respect.

With every burgeoning metropolis comes the need for bicycle messengers. They have the ability to weave in and out of traffic, ride on sidewalks, and take short cuts. They're daring, bold, underpaid, and most are at least half (if not all the way) crazy. And they definitely don't give a shit about what they're picking up or dropping off. They view most of the clients as bureaucratic zombies, and except for a few artistic operations, most customers get little respect. It's ironic, but I can think of no system more under-qualified for transporting important corporate documents than one reliant on grungy, disgruntled bikers.

Six weeks romping around Australia's Tasmanian bush leaves little room for being impressed by a grey Midwestern steel town, but eight hours a day winding through the slalom I grew up in yet barely knew turned out to be fun beyond my wildest imagination. As a rider, I learned pretty quickly the difference between who I thought I was and who the bike knew I was. It's brutal stuff, riding up a mile-long hill at eight a.m. on a single speed bike with a hundred pounds of paper bungeed into the basket with the temperature near zero and the wind and snow having their way with you. To say I lost my mind on the bike more than once is no exaggeration.

Movement is an effect of time elapsing. Velocity changes our perception. And while the pace of time itself appears to maintain its speed, how we move within that dimension is completely variable. Our reality is committed to forward progression, and there are unlimited ways of playing within that paradox of time within time, movement inside movement. In surfing, the wave controls the speed and direction of board and rider, while the surfer is free to maneuver the board, turning and carving into the wave as much as skill and choice allow.

There is a balance between control and surrender on the wave, a magical combination of free will and absolute fate. Perhaps that is why surfing is considered amongst its frequenters as prayer in motion.

Bicycles, unlike surfboards, rely on the dexterity of the rider to generate movement, balance, and destination. The apparatus and operator melt into one fierce being of flesh, rubber, and metal. The rapidly changing environment must also be taken into consideration as its influence is critical: a rock, curb, car, or pedestrian appearing out of nowhere calls for instinct-like response time to avoid an accident. Like surfing, there must be equilibrium between the unknown and the anticipated that creates a rhythm. This is where one finds freedom, that ecstatic thrill of both purpose and complete emptiness. Maybe it's what Nietzsche meant when he said, "I would only believe in a God that knows how to dance."

Over the course of three years, I worked for two different messenger companies. The first two years were at Triangle, the city's largest company, and later at Ultimate, a small operation started by a former Triangle rider and friend of mine. At times I would be one of only a few, and often the only woman rider in a city with five companies and close to 100 messengers. I was humbled by what separated me from my colleagues, and at the same time found an incredibly powerful space in the solitude. Surely the journey would have been much different if I were just one of many two-wheeled sisters, but destiny is something I stopped trying to figure out a long time ago.

My first day in the city, I got hit. Nothing serious. I coasted through an obscured light at an alleyway. The car was probably doing less than 20 mph when my front wheel tapped its left side; I flew off the seat and onto the street. Once more skilled, it would be the type of situation that was "almost an accident," but first timers always have rites of passage, and I took mine with a grin and a prayer. It was near the end of the day, I was tired, my legs hurt like hell, and I had no idea where I was going or which way the garage was. After I got smacked, my two-way radio went flying and broke when it hit the ground. From a nearby payphone I called into base, and they had one of their truckers pick me up. (They used trucks for long distance deliveries and hand offs into the city to the riders.) I'd been looking forward to this job so much and on my first day, already blown it.

I wanted nothing more than to keep riding. It took me three weeks of calling and stopping by the garage to get hired. Andy Gilch, the guy I had been dating, was a rider there, and it was generally frowned upon to bring in the girlfriend. But I was persistent and they needed riders. I don't give up easily, but I also know when something is a waste of time. If they had to fire me for running a light, I wasn't about to argue. So I let Johnny V, the dispatcher, come over to me as I made my way towards my locker. After making sure I didn't need medical attention, he said, "So I guess you won't be coming back in tomorrow?" I looked up. "You mean I'm not fired?" He shook his head. I smiled and was back the next morning.

Johnny and I would become extremely tight. He was the first person I really considered a mentor. I'd even be accused of being his favorite by some of the guys. "The girl gets all the good calls..." But I was fast and furious and Johnny would scold them, "She got hit on her first day and came back for more!" Oh, I'd get hit quite a few more times. In fact, that first hit would turn out to be the least painful of them all. Pain is indeed a powerful teacher, but after a while we can learn to learn in a different way.

Riders are paid per run, and they want to be holding as many packages as they can get. With the help of a good dispatcher, they are set up strategically to maximize building and ride time, much like a video game where you collect various objects, rescue princesses, and thwart evil overlords while racing around through mazes of all sorts trying to stay alive. Radio protocol, the lifeline to guide you to the next destination, was a chore unto itself, every rider calling in dozens of times a day competing to get through the quickest to get the calls, "Rider 8 to base!" Johnny V would answer me, "Goooo aheaaaad 8-er!" "Yah I'm holding three for uptown, base." "Ok. That's all I got for you right now. Call me clean 8, maybe I'll have something for you coming back down."

Messengers are serious athletes, running on an intensely stressful physical regimen. I would ride 40-80 miles per day, my body constantly in motion, fighting against the elements, negotiating intersections, bus lanes, and the dreaded pedestrian, as well as riding in elevators, climbing stairs, tracking down the person with the package while holding anywhere from one to more than a dozen calls in my bag, and of course making sure they all go to the right place. Though one of the most freeing work experiences, there was still a commitment—the duty of a messenger lies in making sure the message is delivered, and that can be a lot of hard work.

The more stress factors one is exposed to, the more adrenaline the body releases, greatly impacting the body-reality relationship. Exposure to prolonged levels of adrenaline can create a "high" or rush-like effect, where the heart is intensely pounding, and feelings of superhuman powers enhance performance, which serves to assist the body in escaping the stressful situation as quickly as possible. Irritability and "crashing" can also occur when exposed to too much adrenaline. Our stress management delivery system is a trait in the human design that has clearly not evolved as quickly as our environments, which have moved from agrarian to the hustle and bustle of big city life. The constant barrage of stimuli of the 21st century is a far cry from the general quietude of life up until a few centuries ago. This lag in our evolution is precisely what makes cities what they are: adrenaline bubbles. Inside those concrete jungles heart rates pump, minds race, deadlines loom; traffic jams, lunch lines.

Yet we have an inherent need for freedom. We are, after all, animals. My dog lets me know precisely when she wants to go out, and if it weren't for the doggy-door, chances are good that

I wouldn't be typing this now. Confinement is a cruel force to be reckoned with. Like my yoga instructor says when the class is struggling with a difficult posture, "The outer is a reflection of the inner." We cage because we feel caged. The cubicle, let's hope, is a fleeting experiment that generations to come will have only to hear of in stories, much like the ones my grandparents told me about carrying blocks of ice up flights of stairs, because though the concept of self-cooling refrigerators had been conjured, the invention was still years in the making.

The average bank-something-or-other processing floor shares many traits with a factory, though its intellectual rather than manual output eludes an air of sophistication, and its health plans, 401K, and company picnics make the fuzzy grey particle walls seem a little less like the cages they really are. Confused college graduates are lured into these boring dead-end careers where workspace is maximized and creativity is stifled, and though there are hundreds of people literally right next to one another, an incredible feeling of loneliness pervades.

When creative expression is muted, the true nature of the being inside the human begins to die. When the passions that define us fizzle, we settle for what corporations dictate to us, because it's easier than looking square in the mirror and committing to believe in something instead of falling for everything. Maybe it's why our culture fixates on the hyped-up corporate media-made artists, musicians, and (super?)stars. Not because we find them exceptionally talented, but because on some level we recognize the inherent nature of the artist in every human. We cling to what's most accessible, vicariously identifying with something—anything, in order to stay alive. The creative expression of self is not randomly bestowed onto a few individuals, but rather randomly explored by them. It's why we fight to keep art programs alive in our school systems. A parent trapped in the drudge of the 9-5 can only hope their children embrace a future that embraces them. This is something worth fighting for. Oil, I'm not so sure about.

Jonathan Swift, who penned the great tale *Gulliver's Travels*, once wrote, "The want of belief is a defect that ought to be concealed when it cannot be overcome." Like his character Lemuel Gulliver, whose grandiose journey met with disbelief and accusations of insanity, what we stand for and by is what makes us who we are. Gulliver held firm to his truth in the face of rigid adversity, reliving it on the walls of his cell so as not to forget the precious details of his experiences. Naysayers are no match for someone who knows their truth.

The roads we travel meet up and often intertwine, but there is one road unique to each of us, and that doesn't mean go it alone, but rather like Charles Bukowski said, "alone with everybody." What I believe is not an answer to anything, just more questions. Like I learned on the bike, in order to get closer to my truth, I needed to push my comfort levels and keep asking more of myself. Riding up hills in the snow and rain forced me to surrender, as a rider, as a young woman, and as a human-being-something. Those times I resisted were the times I ended up back in a truck getting picked up from an accident. My presence to others, be it a secretary, security guard, or mail clerk, although usually quite brief, often seemed a painful reminder for them of what lay just outside the box they chose to shrink into each morning. Many of them were pleasant and friendly, and many blatantly resentful and uncooperative. It took me years to realize their resistance to me, most of the time, wasn't personal. Never shoot the messenger, the saying goes, for a reason. When the day was over, my work was done. I'd delivered the messages. What they did with them was not for me to decide. All that was left was the final ride back to base, holding an empty bag on my back.

www.jillettinger.com

Life With Mamar

Nikki Cicerani

A few years ago, I woke in the middle of the night. The streetlights peeked through the aluminum blinds of my small Manhattan bedroom, the dust floating like celestial bodies in the glow. I had the feeling that my grandmother was in my room. My eyes adjusting to the partial darkness, I scanned the room for her, discerning the shape of things—the dresser filled with trinkets, my 12" TV with the plastic angel sitting on top, the door to my room slightly propped open. Nothing else. No, for certain there was no old lady smoking a cigarette out my window. I went back to sleep.

The next day I spoke with my sister, Dana.

"I had the craziest thing happen to me last night," I told her.

"What was it?" she asked.

"I woke up in the middle of the night and I thought Mamar was in my room."

"Nik, that's so weird that you would say that," Dana said quietly. "I knew she was in my room last night."

Obviously it would have been strange for Mamar, as we called our grandmother, to have shown up in both of our rooms

35

in the middle of the night. But only because she had been dead for five years. Do I believe she was there? Absolutely.

She will be dead seven years tomorrow, February 13, 2006. A devout Roman Catholic, her faith was one of the things that defined her life. Some of my earliest memories are of the two of us in St. Agnes Cathedral, the church in my hometown of Rockville Centre, Long Island. Sitting back in the pews, my little legs in their thick white stockings and Mary Janes barely dangling over the end of the dark wood bench, I remember how I was indoctrinated into the church. The missal in my lap, I turned the pages as they instructed from the pulpit. A reading, a song, a blessing. Stand, sit, kneel. Sit, kneel, pray. Peace be with you. Peace be with you.

I'd rummage through her purse when I got bored and fish out her Rosaries to play with, and eat her cherry-flavored Pine Brother's cough drops. (She always had cough drops because of a chronic cough from smoking, which would later turn into emphysema, which would eventually kill her. But that wasn't so bad because her soul would go to heaven and be with the Virgin Mary and the Baby Jesus, which is why we were in church in the first place, or so I thought: insurance.) When church was over, we went to Nunley's, the local amusement park, and after that we went to Baskin Robbins. And that was what it meant to be a Roman Catholic to me: a few Our Fathers, a few Hail Marys, a ride on the roller coaster, and some mint chocolate chip ice cream.

Today (February 12), upon on the anniversary of her death, I look around the world and am struck by how much of my life is impacted by the question of what people believe as it relates to religion, and what it instructs that we must and must not do to assure ourselves a place in heaven. The U.S. Supreme Court's balance has recently been undone with the addition of another Roman Catholic judge; will they will compelled to overturn Roe v. Wade, impacting the lives of all women in the United States, to gain access to heaven? Downtown in Manhattan, I ride into and out of Jersey City twice a week on the Path train. I enter at the World Trade Center, and before the Path enters into the tunnel, it shimmies alongside the edge of the crater created by a group of men who believed their religious act of destruction entitled them to 40 Virgins in the afterlife.

As struck as I was by my grandmother's identification as a Roman Catholic, her prayers to the Virgin Mary, and her belief that Jesus could make things better, I am stuck more by who she was and how she lived her life. This is her story, and what it tells me about how to live my life and what happens to us in the hereafter.

Mamar is my mother's mother. The story of her life is not dissimilar to Peter Hamill's memoir, *A Drinking Life*. Irish Catholic girl marries her high school sweetheart. Has trouble getting pregnant, but after nine years of trying has a little girl, my mother. They struggle, money is tight. They drink and smoke and each time he gambles away the month's rent, they have to move out before the landlord comes looking for his rent check. He leaves. Now money is really tight, things are really scary. Some Christmas's she has money for toys and a Christmas tree, some years, she hangs a stocking and fills it with oranges. She kneels in the pews of her church, stares at the crucifix, fingers the beads of her Rosary, and prays to the Virgin Mary to forgive her for her sins and to help all the people she loves. She finds a new man, gets married. They don't tell anyone that he's not her daughter's real father, because it's a sin to have been divorced. My Mamar does not want the other kids at her daughter's parochial school to know her mother's transgressions. Sometimes things are good. Sometimes they are not. They get by. Seventeen years go by, and one day, he leaves, too. Fifty-eight years old, twice divorced, she made a living as a secretary for McAllister Tug and Barge and lived in a small two-bedroom apartment in Bayonne, New Jersey.

Ten years later, when I was eight years old and she was 67, Mamar came to live in our attic, since she really didn't have enough money to live on her own anymore. She was getting older, and there was just us—her daughter's family. We turned our third floor into her room, and she lived with us for the next 16 years, the remainder of her life.

The question of her death was of great concern to me as a kid. After all, life was a party when we were together. From the time I was very little, I would stay with Mamar for the weekend in her apartment in Bayonne. The routine was always the same. We would pull out the sofa bed and watch game shows on it all day, tucked under her electric blanket. I was supplied with endless glasses of Tang, and we cooked fried dough and ate it with powdered sugar sprinkled on top. At night, Mamar would send my sister and I to bed, but give me the instructions that when Dana, four years my junior, fell asleep, I could get up. Then we would play cards and drink tea way into the night, when I should have been asleep.

At each birthday, I would make Mamar ten years younger than she actually was. On her 65th birthday I said she was 55. Even at seven, the idea of death was present, and it scared me. Mamar would not deny that one day she would die, but insisted that it would not be such a sad thing. She would go to heaven, she told me, and be my guardian angel.

In an attempt to comfort me, she gave me a story that she said she read and thought I would like. It was the story of a little girl who loved her grandmother and was afraid she would die. The grandmother assured her that one day, even though she would leave this earth, there was a way to always think of her and have her close. It was through bright shiny pennies. Indeed the grandmother insisted that every time the young girl saw a bright shiny penny, she would think of her grandmother and all the good times they had together, and she would know that she was still there with her. The story, of course, was accompanied by a bright shiny penny in a small glass bottle. And even at seven, the parable was not lost on me.

Life with Mamar was indeed fun. And from life in her apartment to life in her third floor bedroom of my house, very little changed. Her space, all 90 square feet of it, was always a place of joy. There was a big tub in a small bathroom, which of course lent itself to hour-long bubble baths where we were allowed to see just how high we could make the bubbles before they'd spill onto the floor. At Christmas we decorated her bedroom with cheap drugstore decorations—a small plastic tree where we could bend the branches any which way, loose tinsel, and multicolored lights. And in the narrow eight-foot hallway from the top of her landing to her bedroom entrance, there was a flimsy wooden cabinet in which she kept a stash of Mallowmars and jellybeans. She never failed to give joy.

Or find joy in the every day. When we talk of her now, we remember how she watched every New York Knicks game at night with my father. She would take a nap during the day so that she could stay up through the whole game. Dressed in a Knicks sweatshirt and Knicks socks pulled up to her knees, she ate her Mallowmars and yelled for John Starks, her favorite player. In fact, the license plate on her 1984 powder blue Ford Tempo read: STARKS, with a Knicks emblem on it.

Her body gave out, little by little over the years. First she developed melanoma and had two toes removed from her right foot, along with the lymph nodes, which made her right leg permanently swollen. Then her teeth fell out and she needed dentures, which she often forgot on the third floor. It was not uncommon for her to get all the way downstairs and then swear, "Damn it to hell. I left my teeth upstairs!!" In my 16 years living with her, I must have made no fewer than 1,000 trips to the third floor to fetch her teeth. Her arthritis set in, and she would wake up and three fingers of her left hand would be pressed tightly into her palm. She had to cut her nails very short so they wouldn't pierce her skin, and rub liniment oil on them for several minutes to get them to release. And then, because she never could quit smoking, she routinely got pneumonia, each time going to the hospital, never quite returning to the same place as before.

Eventually, the stairs became too much for her, and we had to move her from the third floor to the first, making our den into her bedroom. She never complained. She never regretted. She never lost her faith or sense of humor. Whenever we asked her how she felt, she'd say, "Fine. I feel great. If only I could breathe, I'd be perfect!"

On Christmas morning, 1998, as we sat around after exchanging gifts, my father asked us what our New Year's resolutions were going to be. Starting with my mom, we went around and everyone talked about commitments that inspired us. And then my Mamar went, "Well, it would be nice to live another year to see the new millennium. But I've loved my life," she said, "and I am ready to leave it." She died seven weeks later.

It was time to test years of preparation for this moment. What did I believe now that she was gone? Was she in heaven? The question is ever present in my life—what is this life for? Does any of this matter?

Searching for clues to my own faith, I remembered the day of her wake, and how my mother had slipped her Memorial card in the plastic molding of the light switch above the ceramic lamb we have always had in our kitchen. (Above the lamb is where we put all things that should not be lost or forgotten in my house. I would ask my mother, "Where do you want me to put your jewelry?" And she would tell me, "Put it in the cabinet above the lamb." Money, buttons that fell off and would have to be replaced, important receipts—all of them went in that cabinet.) I remembered just yesterday the words of that card:

> Grieve not,
> nor speak of me with tears,
> but laugh and talk of me

as if I was beside you.
I loved you so
'Twas Heaven here with you.

And here was my answer, what I believe.

I believe our fear of the unknown creates a compulsion for clarity, and that compulsion leads to the writing and enactment of laws and the prescriptive tenets of religions. I believe that our desire to be free of responsibility for navigating situations that call for greater understanding of the unknown simply lead to the hardening of positions around laws and religious tenets that invariably make those who believe and follow them right, and the rest of us wrong.

But I do not believe we will be judged on the day we die by someone who will add up the rules I abided by, and the rules I broke, and decide if he will open the gates of heaven to me. I don't think heaven or the afterlife works like that. No great power can grant me eternal life.

I believe our soul is wholly divisible from our physical selves, but that the laws of science apply equally to both. Energy can neither be created nor destroyed. For our bodies, there is a limited time that they can act as a home to our souls. They will cease to exist in their current form, but they will continue on as another form of matter for an eternity. Our soul is just another form of energy; the energy we tap into and nurture in ourselves, the energy we put out into the world. It can be transmitted through what we do when we have this body for its transmission. So our life, every day, is an opportunity for us to imprint ourselves on the fabric of those that will live beyond us. When our energy lives on, expressed in the lives of others, we have achieved eternal life.

As for heaven, I believe as the Memorial card said: it is in Mallowmars and Tang, long card games late at night when we are supposed to be sleeping. It is in finding the joy and laughter available in each moment. And I believe Mamar is here, in my cup of tea, in my cheap drugstore Christmas decorations, in the joy of my warm apartment on the Upper East Side. I believe my Mamar is here, in heaven, with me.

Dodgeball

Jeff Tamarkin

D odgeball had a different name in my high school. It was
called Kill the Jews.
   In this version, the tough kids, the "hoods" as
they were called by all but themselves, were all gentiles. The
object, for them, sanctioned by sadistic gym teachers cut from
the same cloth, was to throw the ball as aggressively as possible at
the Jewish kids, hopefully not only getting them out but inflicting
severe and permanent damage. To them, the Jews were enemies
to be eradicated: PE class as Auschwitz.
   If you had asked the brutes why this was so, I doubt they
could have concocted a coherent answer. Probably they'd picked
up their disdain from their parents, themselves first-generation,
working-class offspring of European immigrants, mostly of
Italian and German extraction. Whatever the root of their
vitriol, though, here we were, two decades removed from the

end of WWII, and these hooligans had apparently not gotten the message: Hitler and Mussolini had lost. It was a good thing, I suppose, that that there were no Japanese kids in my school.

What I didn't understand was why they were after me, of all people. True, I was Jewish, but I wasn't really Jewish. Religion, from the time I was a child, had meant nothing to me. I had been a non-believer since I was old enough to ponder the greater questions of life, and the fact that I had been born to Jews was, in my mind, sheer happenstance. I was forced to attend Hebrew school, and to prepare for my Bar Mitzvah, but I knew that once it had passed my temple-going days would be over. And they were. I've proudly lived a secular life, wondering why the rest of the modern world is so obsessed with superstitions and hocus-pocus fabricated by ancients who didn't have the knowledge we do today. And why it's worth killing one another over.

I was, I acknowledge, Jewish by birth, raised by parents whose own parents had escaped Eastern Europe during the early part of the 20th century. My grandparents had lost family during the great wars, but they'd kept their faith. Judaism to them was about more than bagels and lox; it was something they practiced, keeping kosher, keeping the Shabbos, attending synagogue. Believing in what the Torah said. Judaism was their way of life, who they were. I respected it in them, even if I didn't care to follow.

My own parents were suburban neo-Jews though. Although they considered themselves staunchly, unambiguously Jewish, they didn't bother with kosher or Shabbos unless my grandparents were staying over and, if backed into a corner, really couldn't tell you what made a Jew different than someone of another religion, other than the fact that they simply were not, for some nebulous reason, like us. Passover was only a big deal at our house if relatives were coming over that year; if not, it was little more than a bigger-than-usual dinner with some more-disgusting-than-usual food. We didn't bother reading the Haggadah, although we slogged through the Four Questions to at least lend a semblance of piety to the affair.

Our entire Long Island neighborhood, for blocks in every direction, was occupied solely by Jewish families: a ghetto of tract houses—those kids that beat on us with the ball lived across some imaginary line where Jews dare not dwell. For many of the Jewish families in our ghetto, the religious component of Judaism was undoubtedly taken quite seriously. We'd see them every Saturday, dressed conservatively, walking to synagogue (no driving allowed). But for my family, my parents, my younger brother and me, Saturday was business as usual: Dad would drive off somewhere on his own to indulge in one of his hobbies. Mom would do mom things. The electricity remained on; no candles were lit. We might even eat Chinese food and order something with pork in it. Without shame.

As the post-'50s Jewish-American subculture flourished, my folks dove in head-first. Mom became an avid Mahjong player. (A peculiarity of Jewish suburbia during that period was an obsession with all things Chinese.) Allan Sherman and Mickey Katz records and the *Fiddler on the Roof* soundtrack were played on our console stereo. We all liked potato knishes, took our vacations in the Catskills.

But the religious part was elusive. My parents conversed with my grandparents in Yiddish, but could not read a word of Hebrew. When they attended temple services—mostly on the high holidays, when it was expected of them, but rarely for regular Shabbos services—they mumbled the prayers, faking their way through as best they could. It was important to be seen as Jews, not so much to be a Jew.

God? Not a topic of conversation at home. I have no idea whether my parents were believers or nonbelievers—the subject just never came up. Not when we celebrated Passover and Chanukah, not when they dragged us kids to temple on Rosh Hashanah and Yom Kippur, not even when I was Bar Mitzvahed. God and the teachings of the Torah were not what being Jewish was all about for us. Though they would never admit it, and

45

identified themselves as Jews first, the truth was that we were American suburbanites before we were Jewish anythings.

Which is why I resented being targeted at dodgeball. I took it personally. I was being accused unjustly.

But I was used to it. That sort of persecution had been part of my life since early childhood, being called kike, Jewboy, bagel. Another Jewish kid in school had once been buried up to his neck in the woods by some neo-Nazis who threatened to come back with a lawnmower. But for me, the tag "Jew" was more of a hidden appendage than anything I wore openly. I was a rock and roll kid. I watched *Gilligan's Island* and *My Favorite Martian*. I went to the movies and malls and diners with my friends and, increasingly as the hippie lifestyle loomed, I didn't know or care if any of those friends were Jewish, Catholic, or idol worshipers. Neither did they. It meant nothing to any of us. Who needed church or temple when you had the Fillmore East? As an avowed atheist, that suited me just fine, and my parents never attempted to push me toward any sort of religious belief. It was work enough for them, I understand now, keeping us alive through the heady late '60s and '70s.

As an adult, I remain an atheist. I prefer to turn to science for answers to the riddles of the universe and, more importantly, I understand that there are some questions that have no answers. I accept death as a finality, life as a brilliant coincidence, and look neither skyward nor two millennia in the past for guidance. I've never been able to buy into the concept of deities for the simple reason that if there is a God, then only one religion at most can possibly have the details right (not to mention that He/She/It can be pretty darn nasty sometimes, and I don't feel like worshiping nastiness), and I don't care to spend my time figuring out which, if any, it might be. For me, Bob Marley had it right when he sang, "If you know what life is worth, you will look for yours on Earth."

Yet I realize now that I remain, and always have been, a cultural Jew. If I had to choose a group with which to identify, it would be the Jews. Not the crazy Hassidim, not the Israelis, not the Jews of my parents' suburbia, but Jews nonetheless. I figure any group that could give this world Woody Allen, Bob Dylan, Sacha Baron Cohen, Frida Kahlo, Joey Ramone, Albert Einstein, Andy Kaufman, Sandy Koufax, Stan Getz, Anne Frank, Carl Sagan, Harvey Keitel, Allen Ginsberg, Emma Goldman, the Three Stooges, Leonard Cohen, Gertrude Stein, and Slash is one I don't mind being tossed in with.

So a year from now, when my son turns 13, he will have a Bar Mitzvah. It won't be a big, expensive, garish one as is the custom among the well-heeled; it'll be more like a small but special party for immediate family and his friends. For several months he will study for it. He will learn about the Jewish heritage and Jewish history and teachings. I feel, and my wife (who is also a non-practicing Jew) agrees, that it's important for him to know his roots. It's something else, just like science, math, and the stories of the pilgrims and the Roman Empire, to learn— he is descended from generations of people who identified as Jews, and he should at least have the backing to decide where, if anywhere, that fits into his own life. Even if his parents have rejected much of it, my son's roots are Jewish. And although he's already proclaimed, on his own, without any coaxing from us, that he doesn't believe in God—"and I'm the only kid in my class who doesn't!"—and though I'd be perfectly fine with him sticking to that belief (or non-belief, as it were), he should come to that conclusion from an educated, informed place.

Besides, he too likes bagels and knishes, and that ain't no Italian food. The kid's a Jew, like it or not.

And if he changes his mind about the God dude at some point in his life and declares that he believes in a higher power, be it Judaism or some other -ism? Well, I'm fine with that too. My only requisite is that he come at his beliefs, one way or another, from all sides, from knowledge and thought and meditation, that he consider the available options and keep his mind open. I've always kept mine open—open to the wonders and mysteries of

47

what do you believe?

existence—and it's served me well, dodgeball thugs be damned.

www.jefftamarkin.com

Where Are the X-Wings?

Jeff Gamble

Following the turn of the new millennium, and more specifically the year 2001, my friend Jason pondered out loud where the spaceships were. "Where are the X-Wings?" he asked in all seriousness. "It's 2001, and there are no X-Wings. What are we doing? We don't even have floating cars yet!"

Jason isn't a child, and his questions were partly in jest. But only partly. He posed the query not because he believed that we would actually have flying star fighters at this point, but because thirty years ago, when we were little kids and *Star Wars* was released, it seemed reasonable to think that the world would be drastically different now. People had already been to the moon. So it seemed possible that there would now be ships other than the space shuttle—a craft that's been hanging around without any significant change since George Lucas introduced us to the Millennium Falcon. Thanks to movies, books, and even government projects and plans, the thinking that people would be traveling through space as freely as Luke Skywalker seemed entirely plausible. Come 2001, though, a year and a number made famous by Stanley Kubrick's visionary film, the world appeared very much like it did in the 1970's. We are no closer to X-Wings now than when Jason and I were little. Tell a little kid today that—aside from more traffic, higher gas prices, and slicker looking vehicles—2036 is going to look a lot like 2006, the kid may very well drop his ice cream cone and start to cry. And why not? The things we say are possible versus what actually happens are frequently two different things altogether.

Putting a cap on what's possible in this day and age is very difficult though. That's not a part of today's culture. The only message we want to hear today is what might be possible, not what isn't. You'll never find any newscaster looking into the camera and saying, "This just in … most of us will be dead before any human ever gets to Mars." People would turn the channel in favor of something more agreeable. You will also never hear any advertisement just come out and tell you, "This is our shampoo and we'd like you to buy it, but don't expect it to change your life." People won't buy the shampoo, especially if another one does promise to. And because of this truth, we have shampoos lining the shelves of our supermarkets, all with the promise to make our lives better. Or sexier. Or younger. Or (insert any desirable adjective here).

As capitalists and consumers, people accept that it's not so much about the reality as it is about the promise. Nobody watches advertisements and says, "Yes! Shampoo X is going to get rid of my dandruff and then get me laid! I'm going to run out and buy some right now!" But we do need to wash our hair. So if somebody is selling shampoo, then we're going to buy it. And if along the way we find ourselves confronted with the complex task of choosing between two brands—one brand promising to get us some ass, while the other one is merely going to get our hair clean—then the decision is foregone.

In 1991, Douglas Coupland wrote a book entitled *Generation X: Tales for an Accelerated Culture*, and it spawned the term "Gen X," which has been applied to describe my generation of so-called slackers and deadbeats. Since that time, the popular media definition of the term has been elaborated and stretched. Gen Xer's can be pretty much described now however you see fit. It's a group of people composed of children of the Baby Boomers, people born in the late 60's or sometime in the 70's. They have no clue what they want out of existence, kind of live an alternative lifestyle, are somewhat detached and disillusioned by society, but are also entrenched in popular culture. They are kind of vegetarians—having convinced themselves that Tofu tastes like something—but they will once in a while hit the McDonalds drive-thru, explaining that "it's comfort food." They think yoga and the Wu Tang Clan make perfect sense together. These are people who sit around on the sidewalks with their skateboards, panhandling for change, but have full-time corporate jobs. They grow soul patches to demonstrate that they refuse to be labeled. They buy odd-looking $400 Gucci eyewear to let everyone know that they don't give contemporary fashion much thought. They drink copious amounts of Starbucks coffee, but are opposed to globalization. They buy older homes as opposed to newly constructed ones because they believe older ones are better crafted, but then go straight to IKEA in order to furnish them. Country music sucks but Hank Williams Sr. and Johnny Cash rule. People from the X Generation want something different, but refuse to be put into a category. In a nutshell, they are confused.

The term applied at one time, but if a so-called X Generation ever really existed, I would argue that it's long gone, swallowed by the "X People." There is no longer a generation of confused, detached young people. Nowadays everyone is confused. The X-Gen term originally hung on a demographic that was being bombed with so much new media that it didn't know exactly how to process it all. They became skeptical and callused from marketing saturation. Eventually though, as the

51

new mediums such as cell phones, the Internet, cable TV, and "all things digital" worked their way into the everyday life of all people, everybody got saturated, not just the kids watching MTV. In order to avoid drowning under a deluge of marketing blitzes and "on sale" signs, every conscious, breathing entity had to become at least a little cynical or wary of all the information being pushed their way.

To demonstrate this, we need look no further than the World Wide Web. It wasn't all that long ago that the Internet was barely a vocabulary word. If you had asked me to explain it to you in 1993, I probably would have told you it was something that somehow made it possible to send your mail through your computer, kind of like Scotty beaming people around in *Star Trek*. That same year, my girlfriend's dad bought a new PC for his home and was looking into this so-called Internet thing, trying to figure out how it worked and whether or not it made sense to get it. (In 1993, this made him a pioneer.) We were discussing it at dinner one night, talking about the possibilities and asking each other questions. The exchange between he and I became animated when our attention turned to the devices needed to make the Internet work on your computer: modems. What did they look like? How did they work? What did 14K mean? We didn't have any answers because we didn't know anybody who had the Internet. At that point there was probably still more people using typewriters than computers, so experts were hard to come by. Because of my lack of computer familiarity, I was convinced that modems were the size of a VCR. My girlfriend's dad, on the other hand, explained how he was under the impression that a modem was, as he put it, "a little robot companion." I never found out what he meant by that.

I got my first email address in 1997 or '98, and even then only about half of my friends had an address as well. Nevertheless, it was at this point that I began to figure out how the web worked, and what was possible. I traveled to Africa in 1999 and 2000, and suddenly I understood just how powerful this tool was. I was using a technology that put me in touch with whoever I wanted, whenever I wanted, as often as I wanted, all with the click of a mouse. And I was doing it from a place where communication would have been a completely different story only a few years prior.

Today, a mere ten years later, the Internet has become so entrenched in my life, I literally can't see how I would operate without it. I'm completely plugged in. Within seconds I'm connected to news, sports, friends, family, shopping, movie schedules, games, weather, travel agents, maps ... whatever I can think of. Most of the work I do is also Internet-dependent. In other words, functioning without it has become next to impossible. Information is now so accessible, so plentiful, so rapidly available, it's no longer a question of where you will find it, or if. It's merely a question of how much you will find, and how much will find you.

Thanks to all this media saturation, for better or for worse there are now multiple takes on everything. On March 2nd, 1962, in Hershey, PA, Wilt Chamberlain's 100-point game was a jaw-dropping, individual output, witnessed only by the people in attendance and the few sportswriters there to cover it. Had it happened today however, the coverage of the milestone would have been dramatically different. With all the various ways to now receive, send, and see information, every microscopic performance can be covered by almost everybody, in every way imaginable. A "nobody" can be made into a hero instantaneously, and a hero can be just as quickly demoted to a nobody. Because of this, Kobe Bryant's mind boggling 81-point output this season couldn't just be 81 points. Within hours, the achievement had been dissected from every possible angle, including all the negative ones. On TV, it was 81 points because he shot the ball every time down the court. In the newspaper, it was 81 points because his teammates suck. On the radio, it was 81 points because the Raptors refused to play defense. On the Internet, it was 81 points because Kobe thinks the world is against him. Et cetera, et cetera, et cetera. Wilt Chamberlain was never seen as an endearing figure by the public or the media, so in some ways he should have considered himself lucky to live in the era that he did.

We now have so many things supposedly created to fill the voids—both real and invented—it's hard to say which side is up. We are no longer thinking about what to deem worthwhile; we are occupied instead by what to filter and what to discard. What's left after that aren't real values, they are things that we haven't figured out what to do with yet. And as more information finds its way into our conscious and subconscious every day, figuring out what's worth keeping—or believing—is becoming lost in the shuffle of the ongoing purging process.

While I was in Zimbabwe in 1999, I had a neighbor who I spoke to from time to time. She was an educated white woman, and while not rich, being white afforded her a certain amount of privilege there. Still, she wanted very badly to leave her country. One day we were talking about this, and she was asking me all kinds of questions about the United States, where she had never been before. She seemed very fascinated with the American way of life, almost intent on moving there at some point if she could. When I asked her why, she explained how she could see that things there were better, that people were nicer, that everything was easier. When I asked her where she got this idea, she offered me a simple answer: "From TV and movies." She was serious.

I assured her that not everything was as it appeared in the movies. I explained that the US has plenty of its own problems, and that more often than not these themes don't end up as plotlines. And if they do, they usually get sorted out by the end of prime time. She wasn't buying it though. "I don't know," she said. "It sure seems pretty nice."

Even my wife, who is from Spain, confirms this. "The United States does a good job of marketing itself," she says. "Growing up somewhere else, you get this picture that life is somehow perfect there. Of course a lot of that comes from the movies and TV."

Is life in America perfect? Far from it. But leave it to movies and TV to help you form an opinion and you're likely to come away seeing a lot of attractive things—things you don't have, but are lured into wanting. Was *Friends* a good show? Sure. Was it realistic to think that the six main characters could maintain their ideal bonds and lifestyle in New York without any significant changes or outside interference from the ages of 25 to 35? I'm almost 35 now, and if my last ten years in and around New York was any gauge, then the answer is not "no," but "hell no."

So within this world of hyper bombardment from the ultra-media stimulus machine, how do we figure out what's real, what's not, and what's worth keeping? The question almost has to be rhetorical because there's no real answer. It's no longer an issue of labeling some smart-mouthed, slacking twenty-something with a generation tag. That smart-mouthed, slacking twenty-something was just the first to react to the new world information-packed environment, and now everybody else is trying to figure out how to deal with it as well.

Stimulus now comes flying at us from so many angles, there's too much to process. Every single marketable item out there is labeling itself as something we need and can't live without. Just how many movies can be "one of the best films of the year?" How many shampoos, razors, and deodorants are going to guarantee us greater sex appeal? How fine can the line be between carefully produced, fictitious "reality" TV and actual reality? It seems there is no line anymore.

But of course shampoos are going to tell us that we'll be sexier if we use them. Of course films are going to fall prey to blatant product placement. Of course a ratings-driven television program isn't just going to broadcast whatever a houseful of people are doing 24 hours a day without first sifting through it all for the best drama. With a bottom line at stake, it doesn't make financial sense to anything otherwise. And the fact is, it's always about the bottom line. That's capitalism coming to fruition. Whether we decide to accept it, believe it, or even make note of it—that's the real issue.

Watching the 2005 Super Bowl last year, I was stunned—or rather, bothered—to see hundreds of screaming fans jumping up and down in front of the stage when Paul McCartney was performing during the halftime show. It wasn't that I have anything against Sir Paul, but I found it absurd to think that there are that many people in their twenties, thirties, and forties who would actually go nuts while listening to "Drive My Car." It might have made sense in if this had been Shea Stadium, 1965, but it wasn't. It was halftime at the 2005 Super Bowl, where everything had been clearly orchestrated. I pointed this observation out to the people I was watching the show with, and one woman protested. "No," she said, "I think they are genuinely excited to be there." I asked her if she would be jumping up and down like the people on TV if she were in attendance. She thought for a minute, but then said no. I asked her if anyone she knew would be that excited. She said no. I asked her if she thought Paul McCartney was the hottest available act for the program. She said probably not. Then I asked her if a legendary—and safe—act like McCartney made sense after the following year's "wardrobe malfunction" with Janet Jackson. She said "probably." I didn't ask her any more questions. I didn't have to. I could see that the sad reality—or lack of—was all sinking in. She stared at the screen for a moment in silence, studying the people as they swayed in unison while the former Beatles' star performed "Hey Jude." Her face looked disappointed, as if I had just killed the Santa Claus myth. I wound up feeling bad.

Due to numerous episodes similar to the 2005 Ameriquest Super Bowl Halftime Show, I have figured out that I'm not equipped to handle this media saturated, carefully marketed world. Label me as you will. All of the ads, the polish, the bells and whistles, and the promises of more sex and sexier lives, have only jaded me to the point where I honestly have no idea what to believe. I look at everything with what is probably an unhealthy level of skepticism now, wary of ulterior motives, general corniness, or the omnipresent "catch." To combat this, I've tried to narrow my universe down to smaller bites: appreciating and maintaining my relationships with friends and family, pursuing my hobbies, and learning the finite rules and subtleties of baseball (although even the number-driven pureness of the sport is now difficult to untangle thanks to steroids).

In Jim Jarmusch's film, *Ghost Dog*, numerous references are made to the Japanese Samurai text, *The Art of War*. In one scene, Ghost Dog (Forest Whitaker) quotes: "Among the maxims on Lord Naoshige's wall, there was this one: 'Matters of great concern should be treated lightly.' Master Ittei commented, 'Matters of small concern should be treated seriously.'" And in the end, I think this is good advice. This philosophy doesn't leave a lot of room to ponder pressing issues—like why we don't have X-Wing Fighters yet—but fortunately people like my friend Jason are on the case. I myself am better off allowing for only the minute things—or more manageable ones—and not dwelling too much on grander issues that are beyond my control anyway. This seems to make more sense to me, regardless of any carefully crafted suggestion the world would like me to believe in.—April, 2006

www.jeffgamble.com

30 Days of Tweet

N. Frank Daniels

I have to go away for a while. Dont know when I'll be back. Thank you in advance for your thoughts and prayers. Talk later.
6 minutes ago Mar 22nd from TweetDeck

She told me to cut her out of my heart. In that moment the last part of me died.
6 minutes ago Mar 22nd from TweetDeck

NOthing is ever what it seems until you realize it was that all along and then it was always that all along. Then you hate your own dumb ass.
8:14 PM Mar 21st from TweetDeck

This article about Elliott Smith is breaking me apart. http://bit.ly/I4vCk
9:45 AM Mar 21st from TweetDeck

RT @TheOnion: BREAKING: Obama On Special Olympics
Gaffe: "Sorry, I Acted Like A Retard"
4:31 PM Mar 20th from TweetDeck

Stop defenestrating yourself! Stop defenestrating yourself!
4:08 PM Mar 20th from TweetDeck

We never learn do we?
8:51 AM Mar 20th from web

TV is the great coddler. Watch while burning. Happy happy
happy.
7:16 AM Mar 20th from web

I thought there was love. What a fool I was. So fucking deluded.
9:57 PM Mar 19th from TweetDeck

RT @DAVID_LYNCH: Thought of the Day: Stress inhibits
creativity.
8:22 PM Mar 19th from TweetDeck

Just saw on COPS that the New Orleans cops call prostitution
a "crime against nature." Uh...pretty sure that crime is all
natural.
6:48 PM Mar 19th from TweetDeck

Everybody, all of us, running around documenting our tiny lives.
Hoping. That what comes next will make it all just the slightest
bit better.
11:56 AM Mar 19th from TweetDeck

Off to bang my head on the job hunt rock.
9:36 AM Mar 19th from web

what do you believe?

@jennybent Um...John Mayer is never amusing. Unless he's getting beaten up.
8:20 PM Mar 18th from TweetDeck in reply to jennybent

I am officially cool. Urban Outfitters is now carrying my book. http://bit.ly/2pKBn Futureproof bee-otches!
6:37 PM Mar 18th from TweetDeck

It is an unbelievably beautiful day in Nashville.
4:06 PM Mar 18th from TweetDeck

@mrxtothaz This would have been funnier if you'd said "Got" lotsa swag. THEN you'd be a swaggot.
4:06 PM Mar 18th from TweetDeck in reply to mrxtothaz

Motherfuck, I want one of these. http://bit.ly/PgtSQ
10:49 PM Mar 17th from TweetDeck

Note to self: Get rich from writing. Step One: Land jet in Hudson River. Step Two: Learn how to fly jet. http://bit.ly/8RWSb
10:32 PM Mar 17th from TweetDeck

"Jesus freaks out in the street/ Handing tickets out for God"
8:58 PM Mar 17th from TweetDeck

I dont care what holiday it is, I always end up depressed. No corned beef or cabbage.
7:28 PM Mar 17th from TweetDeck

"I believe they want you to give in/ Are you giving in 2000 man? (Did you love this world/ And this world not love you?) Are you giving in?"
1:13 PM Mar 17th from TweetDeck

Rote response: "That's terrible. I'm sorry."
12:12 PM Mar 17th from TweetDeck

Last link today (promise). This is THE BEST THING I HAVE
EVER SEEN (Noooo!!!) http://bit.ly/7UhMS
11:40 AM Mar 17th from TweetDeck

For your poor person satisfaction I give you....P. Diddy--or
whatever his name is now--stupefied by a one dollar bill http://
bit.ly/StHto
11:32 AM Mar 17th from TweetDeck

Huh. Results. Apparently you do not fuck with Craig or his List.
Death to scammers!
10:20 AM Mar 17th from TweetDeck

@DAVID_LYNCH Not sure how he doesnt get tired of updating
the weather since it seems to always be the same in LA...sunny,
blue sky, breeze.
10:05 AM Mar 17th from TweetDeck in reply to DAVID_
LYNCH

Forwarding @craignewmark #craigslist some emails from these
bastards.
9:43 AM Mar 17th from TweetDeck

@craignewmark These people are skirting Craigslist rules by
using diff. emails to respond. They dont even use original subject
lines.
9:41 AM Mar 17th from TweetDeck in reply to craignewmark

Girl brought home by the guy I'm renting a room from: "I think
I need to go to the hospital. My ears are bleeding." No visual
confirmation.
9:25 AM Mar 17th from TweetDeck

Does one motherfucker advertising job on Craigslist actually have a job to offer or are they all selling get-rich-quick schemes (disguised)?
9:21 AM Mar 17th from TweetDeck

Some Darby O'Gill and Prodigy to start your St. Patty's Day right. http://bit.ly/9N7Wt
6:45 AM Mar 17th from TweetDeck

Just seen Vanderbilt commercial: "Nashville: The City that put heartache on the map."
11:05 PM Mar 16th from TweetDeck

"So much depends on a red wheel barrow..."
9:41 PM Mar 16th from TweetDeck

One-armed people do have an advantage in that they are a hell of a lot harder for the cops to arrest.
11:29 AM Mar 14th from TweetDeck

That @david_lynch begins his day's tweets with L.A.s weather is making me reconsider everything I think I thought about his films.
11:20 PM Mar 13th from TweetDeck

Just-adopted mantra: Dont think about anything. Dont think about anything. Dont think about anything (all anxieties tranquilized.)
10:07 PM Mar 13th from TweetDeck

You never realize just how rough it is all over until u sit in an apartment with 'normal' people who go to a food bank as a regular practice
11:19 PM Mar 12th from TweetDeck

Nashville job market prepares to make itself my bitch.
8:30 AM Mar 12th from web

Cautiously optimisticizing......
6:05 PM Mar 11th from web

i am officially on a hunger strike. nowhere to go in Nashville. and
i have foodstamps. but this situation has gone on too long.
11:34 PM Mar 10th from web

Preparing for the BASE jump into the possibilities of Nashville.
There will be a soft landing. I believe. I BELIEVE.
12:11 PM Mar 10th from web

Out to take the 3 mile stroll to Book Soup. If you see me and
have access to a plastic Oscar replica, feel feel to grab me.
6:35 PM Mar 9th from web

L.A. is way too bright.
12:48 PM Mar 9th from TweetDeck

Nashville forecast: 10 days of rain, cold. SO...drunk in my
underwear, reading in 9 hrs. Not much else to do but wait eh?
Facing Fate scary.
11:31 AM Mar 9th from TweetDeck

In panic mode. Was just told my living plans in Nashville have
fallen through. Homeless in 32 hours. Suggestions?
8:54 AM Mar 9th from TweetDeck

Only Midnight in L.A. So hows come I'm still unbearably
exhausted...and fighting sleep?
1:55 AM Mar 9th from web

@Trulyunaltered Ledger's performance in Candy is pitch-perfect, 'specially when compared with his Joker portrayal
1:37 AM Mar 9th from web in reply to Trulyunaltered

"At half past two; about time to leave/ Drinking champagne from a paper cup/ Is never quite the same/ As i'm waiting around for you..."
1:35 AM Mar 9th from web

Was just chastised for crossing without a walk signal by a man with a blinking l.e.d. in his nose ring. 'Nice job jaywalking chief.'
9:44 PM Mar 8th from web

In L.A. at a hotel on Sunset right next to an In-n-Out Burger of all things. The Dude abides.
8:56 PM Mar 8th from TweetDeck

For all my fellow bibliophiles out there: your featured orgasmatron
http://bit.ly/11JHD3
7:24 PM Mar 7th from TweetDeck

Ride acquired from LAX. Thanks to all of you for stressing on my behalf. Next on agenda: secure living arrangement in Nashvegas before Tues.
5:12 PM Mar 7th from web

"You were the girl who seemed to own the world/ Everything was about you/ And everything was in hyper-jinx/ Just like an old-time movie"
10:16 AM Mar 7th from web

"Well, what if there is no tomorrow? There wasn't one today."
10:05 AM Mar 7th from web

I need a ride from LAX on Sunday to my hotel on Sunset Blvd. I can pay $25. Incentive: I am sort of famous. And 25 bucks. So theres that.
10:58 AM Mar 6th from web

Been listening to Death Cab on continual loop for the last 3 hrs, pulling hair out over logistics of getting to/from L.A. reading.
10:48 AM Mar 6th from web

Unbelievably ill. Spent over 5 hrs in 30 degrees BUT met Bill Murray, Bobby Duvall, that kid from Slingblade. i liked the way he talked.
4:50 PM Mar 4th from web

Preparing for 4 a.m. call time in extra role as "working class writer" in 1930s Bill Murray period piece GET LOW--with mustache, Pics later.
11:52 PM Mar 3rd from TweetDeck

"Losing love is like a window in your heart/ Everybody sees youre blown apart."
2:18 AM Mar 3rd from web

Movie shoots are bullshit. GET LOW-balled.
7:48 PM Mar 2nd from TweetDeck

Funny how being sick is a kind of real low-feeling high.
2:38 PM Mar 2nd from TweetDeck

Have resorted to playing 'the passout game' to kill the insomnia but keep waking back up
2:04 AM Mar 2nd from TweetDeck

RT @mrxtothaz: http://...com/bup6fb And the guy watching the porn did an on camera interview. They showed a closeup of his hands!
11:27 PM Mar 1st from TweetDeck

@caseylee I wish I'd written it. Its from a James Joyce story called 'the dead.' Read the last paragraph: http://bit.ly/LWplY
5:47 PM Mar 1st from TweetDeck in reply to caseylee

"His soul swooned slowly as he heard the snow falling faintly through the universe and faintly falling, like the descent of their last end."
5:40 PM Mar 1st from TweetDeck

March1 in ATL and snowing HARD. It's opposite land! Ready to wake up anytime now....
12:26 PM Mar 1st from web

Huh. Turns out we fucked up the Garden of Eden by trying to stay there. Implications GALORE. http://bit.ly/vjGfP
11:57 PM Feb 28th from TweetDeck

PBR--the 'beer' that keeps on stomping your eyeballs long after the last drop.
10:24 AM Feb 28th from TweetDeck

about to watch Bass Drum of Death @ Star Bar. 'If you die i will kill you'
9:16 PM Feb 27th from mobile web

Holy shit! Just realized I actually made it to 5 without going off on somebody. Jedi training=working. AA=not so well.
4:09 PM Feb 27th from TweetDeck

I'm at my best when I'm at my worst. Thats what she said anyway.
3:53 PM Feb 27th from TweetDeck

Going back underground. Fuck this asskissing shit. Wasnt cut out for it in the first place.
2:42 PM Feb 27th from web

Great interview with Dogmatika just hit the web. Take a read. http://bit.ly/IKt7
12:41 PM Feb 27th from TweetDeck

See, this is what happens when the idiots arent running the asylum: typical bullshit for another bullshit day. I feel fuckin sick.
10:55 AM Feb 27th from web

Success wants to be around success. And vice versa. Easier to live with yourself I guess.
12:48 AM Feb 27th from web

2nd hardest thing I ever had to do: control emotions (Jedi-style). 3rd: survivalism training. 1st: endure isoloation (not in that order).
1:01 PM Feb 26th from web

It's 2:57 a.m. EST. Who needs another drink?
1:59 AM Feb 26th from web

the real test is maintaining composure even while being painted... look ma, no brush strokes
12:41 AM Feb 26th from web

i'm done double dipping. this shit has gotten ridiculous. just ludicrous beyond words.
11:34 PM Feb 25th from web

ever get the feeling youve been cheated?
11:25 PM Feb 25th from web

Everytime you think you have a handle on things then you realize youre holding the pan and its hot as fuck.
10:50 PM Feb 25th from web

Fave lit quote ever: "She would have been a good woman if it had been somebody there to shoot her every minute of her life."
12:27 PM Feb 25th from web

it was pointed out to me that i am what i always wanted to be. that has to count for something.
12:07 AM Feb 25th from web

trying to embrace the ache.
9:54 PM Feb 24th from web

Now: out conquering the world of industrial finance. Later: the whores.
2:34 PM Feb 24th from web

Its 4 o'clock and I am late for beer.
3:05 PM Feb 23rd from web

Whoever said 'It's good to want things' was a sadistic bastard.
11:54 AM Feb 23rd from web

jesus christ who thought it would be a good idea to have huge jackass host the oscars? worst. episode. ever.
10:25 PM Feb 22nd from web

Deadmau5: Best club music in years
5:19 PM Feb 22nd from web

Creative Loafing ATL: Fuckheads extraordinnaire (not you David Lee Simmons--the place went to hell after you left)
5:18 PM Feb 22nd from web

The Oscars: Who gives a shit anymore.
5:17 PM Feb 22nd from web

about to watch mad men and wish i could smoke in dr.'s offices and elevators. smoked in a non-smoking hotel room over the weekend though...
5:52 PM Feb 21st from web

www.myspace.com/nfrankdaniels

Vision is the Thing

John Marshall Roberts

How was Gandhi able to lead India to independence from the British empire? How was Abraham Lincoln able to effectively abolish American slavery? How was Martin Luther King able to help lift our country from the depravity of southern racial segregation? How has Barack Obama managed to shift the red/blue electoral map of the United States to so many shades of ever-inspired purple?

Traditional historians and pundits have sought to explain the successes of these fallible heroes with mundane analyses involving unique personal attributes, contextual historical antecedents, and emerging social trends.

But forget all that stuff. It's irrelevant. Facts are always an afterthought...

Vision is the thing.

Transformational leaders are flawed humans, just like us. But, unlike most of us, they are gripped by a compelling vision. In this vision, they see a future in which the constraints and sufferings of the present moment will be completely unnecessary. Through this vision, they know that all humans are bonded eternally on a plane that defies reason, and that scarcity of any kind is always a matter of collective choice.

Vision isn't rocket science, it isn't brain surgery, and it isn't wishful thinking. Vision is absolute clarity into the unseen order of things. Transformational leadership is the willingness to let that unseen order emerge by surrendering the rotting scraps of ego-comfort that would keep us in chains, that a transcendent new purpose might express itself through our humble hands.

Authentic vision always breeds a deep sense of gratitude and awe. And I can guarantee you that these great visionaries—Gandhi, Lincoln, MLK, Obama, and all of those who came before—have stood in wonder at the powerful forces working through them. What's more, every single one of these transformational figures would be quick to remind us that we have the exact same power at our disposal, should we be willing to accept it.

www.jmarshallroberts.com

What I Believe

Azikiwe T. Chandler

"If you would know God, look about you and you shall see Him playing with your children. And look into space; you shall see Him walking in the cloud, outstretching His arms in the lightning and descending in rain. You shall see Him smiling in flowers, then rising and waving His hands in trees."

— Kahlil Gibran

Just as footprints are evidence of the existence and movement of life forms, the universe is evidence of Divine Creative Energy.

The beauty of biology, awe-inspiring forces of nature, the harmony of the universe, the myriad of colors, shapes, patterns, and designs that surround us … that are within us provide proof that there is a Divine Creative Energy responsible for the existence of the universe. Life and the universe function too impressively for all that we know to have happened by chance. I am inclined to believe that there was a "big bang" out in space that set in motion the process of evolution. The big bang had a cause; there must have been a cause for the big bang to have taken place. Divine Creative Energy is the cause; it is the life-force which created the universe. It is the beginning of all things.

Just as a baby carries the life-force of its parents, so does Divine Creative Energy flow through all of creation. And just as a parent wants the best for its child, so does this Energy want what is best for the universe. I believe in an omnipotent, omniscient, benevolent Divine Creative Energy.

Since it is human nature to want to personify this Energy, more definitive nouns like "Creator" or "God" are more appealing to us. Such words help us visualize something to which we can relate. However, just as a baby in its mother's womb has no concept of its mother's face or the life-force which envelops and sustains it, so are we in darkness as to the true appearance and nature of Divine Creative Energy. Nevertheless, for simplicity's sake, I will henceforth use the words "God," "His," and "Her" to refer to Divine Creative Energy.

My siblings and I really didn't grow up with any particular religion. My father went to Catholic school when he was younger, and my mother went to church while growing up in Summerville, South Carolina. I'm not sure if it was a conscious decision on their part, but I appreciated not having to go to church every Sunday.

That is not to say our house was without spirituality. My fondest memory of Sundays was waking up to the John Coltrane and Miles Davis records my father played on the stereo, while mom cooked a breakfast of grits, eggs, and turkey bacon. Jazz was the intro to and segued between speeches by Malcolm X, Marcus Garvey, and Booker T. Washington.

The entire family would later leave the house in support of the Ebony City Soccer Club Lil' Peles. Mom and Dad coached, while my siblings and I played. In the evening, after consuming another of mom's healthy home cooked dinners, we'd play Scrabble while listening to the message filled music from artists like Bob Marley, Burning Spear, Steel Pulse, and Linton Kwesi Johnson.

Our Sunday routine instilled in me a sense of spirituality that celebrated family, art, healthy living, community, and liberation theology. The essence of this spirituality can be summed up in one word: love. When we love, we always try to improve ourselves, and that's when everything is possible. Familial love blossomed at the breakfast table and game board to help maintain unity in the family. As Coltrane's and Davis's pursuits of excellence in their craft took music to new heights, their dedication (i.e. love) demonstrated love's transformative power. Exercising emphasized that a healthy love for self makes us stronger, just as being a part of the Ebony City Soccer Club manifested a communal love that strengthened the community. The civil rights speeches gave us modern examples of a love of justice so selfless that the speakers gave their lives to uplift the oppressed.

Still, from time to time my parents struggled with the lack of religion in our life. They sometimes acquiesced to friends' offers to take us to church. I liked the Quaker Meetings and Unitarian Church I attended a few times, but aside from the singing, I did not appreciate the "holier than thou" churches that tried to convert me as soon as I walked in the door.

"Now is the time in our service when we like to recognize the visitors to the church," the reverend would say. "Please stand if you are new to the church, and let the congregation know what church you are a member of."

The "stand and reveal" sessions seemed to end quite harmlessly. That is, until I realized that they were precursors to the "come and get saved!" part of the Sunday morning routine.

Invariably church announcements (or something else) would follow "stand and reveal," but everyone knew that "come and get saved!" time was right around the corner. Once they found out that I wasn't a member of any church, they had the green light.

"If you've ever been a sinner! If you've never invited Jesus into your heart! If you've been a liar or a cheat! If you want salvation from your unholy ways!" The preacher would continue until he had whipped the church into a frenzy. (At least one person always caught the holy ghost.) "We'd like to invite you to turn your life around right now! You need to be saved if you wanna go to heaven!!"

I remember being twelve years old and sobbing uncontrollably as I ran to the front of the church to be saved because I was convinced I was otherwise a sinner doomed to rot and burn in hell.

Who knows, I might have stayed saved had I not seen the reverend stumbling home drunk and belligerent one night. I remember thinking to myself: "That can't be right. How can he lead me to salvation when he's not living a pious life himself?" That's when I realized that no hypocritical clergymen could be certain about the nature of God and His intentions for humanity. Furthermore, I began to question the necessity of other human beings serving as intermediates between God and myself.

I recognize and appreciate the positive effects religion has played in the personal lives of people. The Nation of Islam transformed the criminal-minded Detroit Red into the self-educated Malcolm X, who inspired countless African Americans to improve themselves. As a child I didn't like to go to my grandmother's house because I knew there would be a lot of alcohol, profanity, and cigarettes—a combination that inevitably led to someone getting slapped upside the head, and I didn't want it to be me. Since my grandmother became a Jehovah's Witness, she has given up the lifestyle that I found so scary.

While I recognize the positive influences of religion on humanity, I think the negative effects of religion far outweigh the positive ones.

Since I believe in a benevolent God, I can't imagine Him appearing to one group of people saying, "OK, you guys will call yourselves Jews. Now go over their and kick some Muslim ass!" Then to another group, "Now, you are my conquistadores. Your job is to destroy entire civilizations in newly discovered lands." And to another group, "Hey Catholics, I'm tired of those Protestants! Bust some heads over there in Ireland for me!" Religion was used to justify everything from the Crusades and slavery to 9/11 and the invasion of Iraq. Warfare, slavery, and death are byproducts of religion. They cannot be God's plan for humanity. Religion is a construct of human beings used to manipulate and control other human beings.

That is not to say that God does not interact with us. On the contrary, Divine Creative Energy envelops us. It is omnipresent. It flows through every living thing. If we open our hearts and minds we can learn God's plan by contemplating how bees and flowers interact. However, since people sometimes need literal examples which look more like us, God sent humanity human examples that could role model His plan for us. I believe all of the human beings around whom religions were created did indeed walk the earth. Just as some children look more like their parents than others, these individuals were uniquely in tune with the purest form of the Divine Creative Energy that flows through all of creation.

With their amplified Divine Creative Energy (i.e. Godliness) constantly radiating from them, the messengers were so beautiful that human beings fell in love with the messenger at the expense of the message. Those who came in contact with this Energy were so awed that they shared the experience with others through word of mouth. People got together and decided to help spread the message. In some instances the message was pure and accurate. In many instances they were biographies written over hundreds or thousands of years, fraught with author interjections that changed the messages significantly. Analogies and parables were created, intending to make the message clearer. Some additions did clarify things; others complicated matters worse, leading to further misinterpretations. Soon entire books were created about the life and times of the messengers and their teachings. All of a sudden religions were formed around each messenger. But with countless stories and authors, confusion was inevitable. When people didn't agree with one account, they created their own accounts. Further separations ensued. So rather than creating the unity of which the messengers spoke, humanity became lost in the confusing texts and documents produced centuries after the messengers left earth.

Nevertheless, if you strip away all layers added by humanity, and get down to the purest kernel of truth brought by each messenger, the message was always the same: Love one another.

"Let no man do to another what would be repugnant to himself." — Krishna, 3000 BC. Mahabharata 5:5-7, Bhagavad Gita (Hinduism)

"What is hateful to you, do not to your fellow man." — Moses, 1400 BC. Talmud:Shabbat 3id, Torah (Judaism)

"That nature alone is good which refrains from doing unto others whatsoever is not good for itself." — Zoroaster, 1000 BC. Dadistan-I-Dinik 94:5, Zen Avesta (Zoroastrianism)

"Hurt not others in ways that you yourself would find hurtful."— Buddha, 566 BC. Udanavarga 5:18, Dhammapada (Buddhism)

"Do not do to others what you would not like yourself." — Confucius, 530 BC. Analects 12:2 (Confucianism)

"Do unto others as you would have them do unto you." — Jesus Christ, 30 AD. Luke 6:31, Bible (Christianity)

"No one of you is a believer until he desires for his brother that which he desires for himself." — Muhammad, 622 AD. Sunnah (Islam)

"Blessed is he who prefereth his brother before himself." — Baha'u'llah, 1863AD. Tablets of Baha'u'llah, p.71 (The Bahai Faith)

Many faiths teach of an afterlife, which they often refer to as heaven or paradise. Ministers of these faiths teach us that if we are good on earth we will be rewarded with paradise. On the other hand, if we are not good on earth we will be condemned to a fiery hell.

No one knows for certain whether there is an afterlife, but I think God's plan is evident in the statements above. If we truly loved one another, and practiced this love through our actions; if we realized that all things are interconnected and saw ourselves as citizens of the world, instead of being territorial and nationalistic, we could create a paradise here on earth! That's God's plan!

Take Jesus for example. If he were the embodiment of God's love for creation, believing in that Love would lead to salvation of the earth! There is enough food to feed everyone. We have the technology and capabilities to clothe and provide safe housing for all human beings. There is no reason why humanity can't eradicate the death and destruction plaguing so much of the world.

On the other hand, practicing nationalism leads to global warming and warfare as wealthy militaristic nations steal and hoard the resources (e.g. trees in the Brazilian Amazon and oil in Iraq) of poorer nations. As global temperatures rise and the threat of bombs (whether nuclear or "dirty") loom overhead we risk creating hell on earth.

I'm not sure I believe in a devil. It's too pessimistic for me. Humanity has gone awry due to greed. Not malicious greed. In fact, it is a greed borne out of love—indeed, a selfish, narrow-minded love, but love no less: the love for an individual's family, those that are closest to him.

Our animalistic nature dictates that our primary goal is to ensure our own survival. The secondary goal is to ensure the survival of our family. In adhering to these goals we ensure the survival of the species. This is the law of nature.

We've evolved into creatures with a seemingly superior intellect to that of the rest of the animal kingdom. The messengers were sent to teach us that we can evolve from animalistic beings to spiritual beings by expanding our love for self and family to that of all of humanity and nature. We can transform this planet (and perhaps the universe) into a paradise where no one goes without food or shelter. If love were the order of the day, all needs would be met, and there would be no need for crime or warfare. We'd realize that all things are interconnected and that we cannot cause destruction in one part of the world and not expect to feel the effects of that destruction in other parts of the world.

I'm inclined to think of God as a watchmaker. The Divine Creative Energy which set evolution in motion in such a way that He would not have to be involved with the day to day lives of each entity every second of every day. That is not to say that He couldn't be involved with everything every hour of every day. If Divine Creative Energy is omnipotent, omniscient, and omnipresent, It can do all things. Indeed, It is all things, but I digress.

Consider the healing process of the human body. After the skin is cut, blood rushes to the site of the injury and immediately begins to coagulate. Soon there is a scab; a natural band-aid that protects the wounded area until the healing process is complete. The scab falls away when it is no longer needed. That is a brilliant design! Consider how dead life forms fertilize the ground facilitating the growth of new life. That is excellence in design! There is a master plan at work, a supreme balance so brilliant we can't possibly completely understand it in its entirety.

But we do have a role to play. We will either be residents and caretakers of our paradise, or we will be fertilizer for new life.

Watches sometimes need repairmen. They have to be tweaked from time to time. God is not fallible in his design, but in allowing human intellect to evolve to a point where we can govern ourselves, He's also given us the ability to stray from His plan. Perhaps the parent to child analogy would be better ... At any rate, as illustrated in the quotes above He has sought to put us back on course time and time again.

Not only does God communicate with each of us through exemplary human beings like Buddha and Dr. Martin Luther King, Jr., He also communicates with us through friends, family, and strangers, as well as through signs.

A seed buried deep in the earth receives a sign that it is time to sprout when the earth around it warms in the spring. Likewise, there are frogs that lie dormant for months, until they receive a sign in the form of torrential rains, which make it possible for them to emerge from their earthen confinements.

Very rarely do I pray, for I believe that an omniscient God knows my heart and desires. And my earnest work and actions are in themselves prayers. For example, rather than pray for peace on earth, I work towards creating such peace in myself and teaching youth to solve conflicts peacefully. These actions are my prayers.

Sometimes however, like all human beings, I have questions and wonder whether I am headed down the right path. Such was the case a couple of years ago when I found myself wondering if I should keep leading groups of youth on experiential learning trips or proceed to graduate school.

Below is an account of a sequence of events illustrating how I believe God was communicating with me. They took place during a jeep safari that my group and I were experiencing in Bolivia. The description is a letter I sent to friends and family shortly after the safari.

Salar de Uyuni y el altiplano, Bolivia (2/16/04 – 2/19/04)

"God created the world so that, through its visible objects, men could understand his spiritual teachings and the marvels of this wisdom."
— Paulo Coelho

Yes, it's cold at 16,000 feet above sea level, but the beauty of thousands upon thousands of flamingoes strutting in a fiery red lake and flashing their brilliantly colored wings is enough to make this summer baby from steamy Charleston, SC, forget about the cold and lose himself in the scene.

The Altiplano is another world, reminiscent of landscapes you've scene in *Star Wars* and *Star Trek*: miles and miles of desert with snow-capped mountains and volcanoes, strange rock formations that remind you of Salvador Dali paintings ... I cannot do justice to it here (you may want to Google to find pictorials) ... We saw thousands of domesticated llamas grazing the plains. Their tagging (red yarn attached to their ears and neck) and fluffy fur makes you want to personify them. You get the impression that they think they're better than their distant cousins, the wild vicunas that also roam these plains. The viscachas—which are somewhat tame due to the amount of tourists that stop by their rocky hiding places to offer them food—remind you of rabbits, but they have shorter ears, longer tails, and are much more agile due to their environment.

We arrived at Laguna Verde ("Green Lake") after visiting the geysers and hot springs. It appeared to be more brown than green, but our guide informed us that the water only turned green when the wind picked up and stirred the copper and other sediments resting at the bottom of the lagoon. We waited for about 30 minutes, and you could actually see the water begin to change at the far side of the lake. It was like magic, the way the murky lagoon transformed into a bright aqua marine blue-green Caribbean sea right before our eyes!

And I have NEVER seen as many stars as I did from

the dormitory at Laguna Colorada. I was impressed by those I saw while camping in the big sky states of New Mexico and Colorado as an AmeriCorps-NCCC Team Leader back in '95, but here the sky was FULL of stars. They were so bright and brilliant that they seemed close enough to touch ... Made me wish I had studied astronomy at some point so I could tell what was what. It's no wonder ancient civilizations were more in touch with the universe; you can't help but be intrigued and enticed to interact with celestial bodies when you see them so clearly, night after night.

The salt flats, and in particular La Isla Pescado, were the icing on the cake. I only had three shots left on my disposable camera, and I wanted to save at least one of them for the hotel made out of salt that we would be visiting later. So I was hiking this island of thirty-foot cacti looking for the perfect shot to capture the beauty of this oasis in the middle of hundreds of miles of bright white salt, when I was moved to sit and meditate. I was overwhelmed by a sense of awe and appreciation for the Creator and creation ... There were no words, but God was speaking to me. I was filled with an abundant sense of joy! It was a sensation that I doubt I will ever forget.

Over the past several days I had been entertaining doubts about whether I was on the path to fulfilling my destiny or wasting time "gallivanting around the world." I was really enjoying my travels, and was thinking of postponing grad school again in order to spend more time traveling. I was 32, past the age where society says that people should be serious about their lives. My main question was, "Am I doing the right thing?" The sensation I felt on the island was akin to the quote below.

"Listen to your heart. It knows all things, because it came from the Soul of the World, and it will one day return there ... no heart has ever suffered when it goes in search of its dreams, because every second of the search is a second's encounter with God and with eternity." — Paulo Coelho

A few weeks after the experience on Isla Pescado I received another communiqué from God. The poem at the end of this missive sums up my personal relationship with the Divine Creative Energy that I refer to as God. In a nutshell, it illustrates what I believe.

The Dream, The Poem, and The Epiphany (March 9, 2004)

I believe that dreams are the language of God. When God speaks in the language of the soul, our dreams contain messages that we must interpret. I had a dream while in the rain forest of Bolivia that lead to an epiphany that my next major objective must be writing a book.

The Dream

I was attending a poetry night at friend's locale in Charleston, SC. There were no more than twenty people in what appeared to be a small café, when the owner asked if I would read something. I agreed, and he told me that I would be up in an hour in the next room. In the meantime I sat at a table familiarizing myself with the poem he gave me.

Forty-five minutes later I am escorted into a larger room packed with 100 people facing a stage on which a jazz quartet is tuning their instruments.

The DJ/owner asks the crowd to welcome me and another young lady to the stage. It dawns on me that I am the emcee. So I thank the owner for setting up the affair, thank the band for providing musical vibes, thank the crowd for coming, and hype them up for a beautiful night of poetry and jazz.

The young lady begins to read the poem, but she is stumbling over the words, and the crowd is grimacing. I discreetly ask her and the crowd if I may take a crack at it. Everyone agrees that it's alright.

Upon receiving the young lady's copy of the poem, I realize that there is an introduction to the poem, and begin to read it. But I am also stumbling through the words. Then I realize that this version of the poem is written in Portuguese.

I beg the crowd's patience as I search my pockets for the English version of the poem, explaining that while I speak Spanish and Italian, I do not yet speak Portuguese.

Finally, I find my English version, but just as I am about to start reading, I wake up.

Normally I would consider this an anxiety dream having to do with my worrying about whether or not I am performing well (e.g. work wise, etc.), but I felt invigorated, despite waking up in the middle of the night in the jungle! The sensation was akin to the one I felt on Isla Pescado in the salt plains! This was a sign! God communicating with me! All of a sudden I realized that I had to write my book!

REWIND: Thirteen days prior to this dream I found a poem that I had started three years and one month ago. It was a poem that I had never finished. After reading what I had started, the rest of the words came to me. (Peep the fact that thirteen represents transformation, a new beginning.)

What was most interesting about this incident was the fact that I haven't written poetry in quite a while, and that I was feeling particularly low at the moment that the words came to me...

FAST-FORWARD back to awakening in the middle of the night after my dream. Here's my interpretation:

Chilling in the small café, I am vibing with the other attendees of the poetry night: I've been comfortable sharing my stories with many small groups (e.g. the one with which I am currently traveling) for quite some time now.

Being invited by the Owner to read something to a larger audience: The sensation I felt on Isla Pescado was that traveling is what I am supposed to be doing. That I should not doubt it, or fight it, but embrace it and roll with it. It is God saying "Travel, and share your stories with the world."

My co-emcee stumbling through the poem: I may be on stage with someone else, but ultimately this task is my responsibility, and I must see it through.

Not understanding Portuguese: 1) My travels are not done. I have other languages to learn. 2) Right now, I must speak in my own voice. 3) It's an obvious reference to Paulo Coelho, one of my favorite authors (who is Brazilian).

Waking up before reading the poem: My own voice is the reality of this poem that God helped me finish, not a dream. Furthermore, I have to continue striving to make my dreams reality.

Counting Blessings (February 25, 2004)
(A work in progress)

This could be a poem about despair. Of living here and there, but being nowhere.

I could speak of longings and desires and smoldering fires. Of being broke, feeling sick, and not having shit. I could speak of places I've never seen, or not meeting the woman of my dreams. I could speak of racism and misogyny and police brutality...

But I'd rather speak of travels, good food, and having the right attitude. I'd rather speak of following dreams and other good things like the joys that life brings. How about sunrises and sunsets, and having no regrets?

I mean: I'm a happy brother. Raised by a loving father and mother who instilled in me wisdom, courage, AND serenity. As well as the gumption to create my own reality.

"I can fly high like a bird in the sky."

So I can speak to you of my renaissance in Italy. And beautiful waterfalls in Hawaii. Of soaking in heavenly hot springs in Costa Rica, and skanking to reggae in Jamaica. I can reminisce about Florence and its magnificent dome. Or finding a home with Italians, Greeks, and Africans in Rome. Of Bolivia and the mystical island rising out of its great salt plains. Or of being eight years old and learning to take pride in my name.

I can speak to you of being fluent in two foreign languages. Or how not knowing the future no longer causes me anguish. Ti puedo hablar sobre cuanto me gusto viajando por Centro America. O posso dirti quanto mi piace la cucina Italiana.

I can speak to you of the exhilaration of snowboarding down snowy peaks, and the majestic wonder of diving the ocean deeps. Of playing soccer in seventeen countries, and of having many friends but no enemies.

This is a list that goes on and on, but for brevity's sake I'll cut it off here to keep the poem from droning on too long...

The point is that I've had a few dreams fulfilled. And I thank God because I know it's Her will. She's spoken to me many times through many signs. And I've vowed to keep an open mind, and enjoy Her reason and Her rhyme.

I have no time for staring at closed doors, or falling into any kind of depression. I'd rather thank Her for life's lessons, and count my many blessings. I am grateful for Her loving kindness. And I will always light a candle rather than curse the darkness.

"A human being is a part of a whole, called by us 'universe', a part limited in time and space. He experiences himself, his thoughts and feelings as something separated from the rest ... a kind of optical delusion of his consciousness. This delusion is a kind of prison for us, restricting us to our personal desires and to affection for a few persons nearest to us. Our task must be to free ourselves from this prison by widening our circle of compassion to embrace all living creatures and the whole of nature in its beauty." — Albert Einstein

—Korea, January 31, 2006
www.azikiwe-chandler.blogspot.com

For The Moment

Andrew Gandolfo

What do I believe? It depends when you are asking. Belief is not a static occurrence. What one believes should change constantly every day, hour, minute, and second of their existence if they are observing, experiencing, and processing life around them. I'm not talking radical change over a short period, though events and experiences in our lives might render a more radical change in what we believe in an instant; the changes I speak of are minute and almost without notice. However, these micro changes in our beliefs, which are caused by our observing, experiencing, and processing, culminates into much larger changes over time.

When the question of what I believe was posed to me, this was the answer that came most naturally. Giving a specific answer of what exactly I believe at this very moment, in my opinion, would be inaccurate and superficial; it wouldn't really be giving justice to such a weighty topic. Instead, I focus on the process that makes up this constantly changing exercise of belief.

If I can liken it to anything, it would probably be similar to the processes of plate tectonics that shape and form our earth over millions of years. As anyone knows, the Himalaya did not achieve their majesty in a short time; it took a humanly incomprehensible amount of time, involving colliding plates, earthquakes, magma, volcanoes, uplift, and all sorts of physical and geological activity that I'm not qualified to get into here. The Himalayas (or any of the world's mountain ranges, geological formations, etc.) are the result of billions of events, big and small, that contribute to what we see today.

The formation of one's beliefs is very similar to this process, though on a human scale. Through the process of living and experience, we observe; we learn from what we see whether we are conscious of it or not. This process of observation and learning through life and our experiences is internalized; tiny bits of information causing the slightest, almost imperceptible change, similar to two plates deep within the earth moving ever so slightly against each other. One cannot detect these changes day to day, neither the ones within us or the ones beneath our feet, but they occur nonetheless, and their impact over time is profound. The experiences that shape our belief vary in size, some much more profound and dramatic than others; the impact of a death of a loved one, the birth of your child, falling in love, perhaps seeing the Himalayas for the first time, all affect our beliefs much more deeply than, say, noticing a new bird perched in the tree outside your window or a surprise snowstorm. This is similar to comparing small plate movements to massive earthquakes that serve to accelerate the geological process, the physical results of which are much more obvious over a shorter amount of time. Significant events in our lives, in a similar way, can serve to accelerate changes in our beliefs. These forces over time, alter our beliefs from one form into something ranging from slightly

88

different to altogether different, much like the forces of the earth have changed the Himalaya from one form many millennia ago into what we see today.

It's important to note that rate of change and the profundity of what changes our beliefs over time varies from person to person; these experiences are extremely relative. That new person you noticed delivering the mail this morning, of possibly little or no consequence in your life, might shake the foundations of what love and happiness is to someone else when they meet this person for the first time; this person might be the earthquake of someone else's ever changing tectonics in their belief landscape. Different forces affect people and their beliefs in different ways; their make-up is different, much the same way the soil beneath one continent is different from another. The tectonics of belief is relative from person to person.

The important aspect to remember is: Try as we might to keep our beliefs constant, the inertia of change is both irresistible and unstoppable, much the way the forces of geology that shape our physical landscape. Change over time should be accepted and embraced, for change is inevitable. With this in mind, it's best to keep in tune with the world around us; pay attention; experience and learn, for it is these events and experiences that are shaping you and your beliefs.

This, at least at this moment, is what I believe.

Logical Magicanism

Sarah Gonek

flights and fogs

The other day there was a thick and mysterious fog over the city
and all the eagles were flying low beneath it right in front of my car
window at 7 am.

As I got off the highway,

I saw a dead one laying on the side of the road and

standing upright on its belly was a living eagle. It gestured with its
beak toward the unseeing eye of the other, then

it seemed like time slowed with my car, and as I approached, it
looked me right in the eye and held my gaze with a

look of such alien sorrow and intelligence.

an anthology of ideas

It felt like we were communicating. Some sort of understanding
between species passed between us.

It was wrenching.

I heard from a friend later that eagles mate for life.

One of the favorite pastimes of human beings is to use
myth as a metaphor for perceived reality. Belief is a
mythology we live by, so in order to talk about my belief,
I'm going to use perceived reality as a metaphor for myth. Once
in a while, reality and myth look a lot alike, but how "true" they
are doesn't seem to matter much to either of them. So for now,
I throw truth out an imaginary window. If it hits someone on
the street below after its defenestration, I humbly apologize, and
dare anyone to prove it came from me in a court of pretend
law.

According to the current bang-style theory, all the initial
particles and waves in our space-time formed very close to each
other from the same "stuff" before spreading out to make our
universe. Particles are constantly appearing and disappearing,
and no one knows where they are going or coming from, or
even if they're different particles. But visualize the beginning
of this universe. Something happens (the bang), suddenly a
massive amount of waves (energy: or, if you like, a bunch of
intangible thinglessness) radiate and spread out. At first, there
was no physical matter at all. I like to think of those first waves
as imaginary fields of potential. So one day, two waves were
flowing around and they bumped into each other. The first wave
apologized; the second was befuddled. It had thought it wasn't
real, but if it had no reality, how could something have bumped
into it? And a fictional something at that! Taken aback, wave
number two (let's call it Eve) said, "Wait, are you real?" Wave
number one replied, "I guess I must be if we just bumped into
each other." After they interacted, they couldn't keep thinking

they were imaginary, so in the place they connected, a figment of "reality" formed: a particle. As you can imagine, a whole bunch of this sort of inarticulate schmoozing went on.

Now the crazy thing about particles is that they are not at all like dust motes. They are actually just places where there is an interaction between fields. Waves are fields. Scientists found this out when they shot a particle at a wave to see what would happen. Even though the wave was a wave as it approached, it turned into a particle at the exact moment they collided! The wave has the potential to BE specifically in any of the locations that it covers. What makes it BE in just one of those places is a connection. A wave of potential becomes actual when coming in contact with something else that was also once a wave of potential, but made a connection and became a particle. So a lot of this sort of thing went on for quite some time, as all the energy kept spreading out, going on dates, making friends, and so on. It was a long, slow seduction, but eventually, a lot of these particles and waves started to form habits. They kept going back to their favorite restaurants, buying the same colored roses, and so many of them kept being drawn to the same spots that they became a place to be. Those habits are what we now think of as matter. Like people, if they hang out long enough, they become solid. So planets and rocks, waters and people (with their own mess of particulars and waves) finally happened. All of these fields of potential kept interacting, and eventually they happened to make self-evolving complex organisms. Existence is like a really big side-effect.

We know from experiments that once a particle has been in contact with any other, they retain a communicative link even over vast distances and times. It's true that particles and waves are constantly appearing and disappearing, so it seems hard at first to call it a network. Here is where we can benefit from using science as metaphor. We can take the system logic of myth and apply it to science. All of the energy that eventually became what we think of as The Universe initiated from the same source. In this quantum metaphor, the initial particles formed in very close proximity to each other. Very close! They came from the same place. Since any particle that comes in contact with another particle maintains a communicative link, all the initial particles had a communicative link. So we have this first web of communicating particles as they spread out. Certainly particles appear and disappear all the time, but retrace it from the beginning. One of the things in this web disappears, but the rest go on. A new particle suddenly appears. At the moment, for something to be considered part of our universe, it has to have had some connection with something else or it would not be a part. It would not be considered any thing at all. So any particle that wants to be part of our universe must come in contact with something else first. As soon as it comes into contact with any other particle, it gains a communicative link with a particle that is in communication with all the other particles. After this has happened once, it can continue to happen indefinitely. All of the particles in our space-time are in communication with each other. And this is the stuff that everything is made out of. Everything and everyone you know is made up of these particles and waves. So at least at a quantum level, we are all connected.

Now here comes the really cool part. We KNOW for sure that our bodies are capable of taking in particle and wave information. That is how we sense—we sense photons, and they tell us everything we see, pick up on sound waves, etc. Our brain organizes the individual disparate bits into something we can understand: words, wind, savory. Granted, this occurs through a vast network of particles and waves, but where is there not a vast network of particles and waves? As a society, we are used to talking about sensations as particles and waves already. We talk about light as particles, sound as a wave, etc. The very idea has seeped into our everyday language.

We are bombarded with a nearly infinite amount of information all the time, and we know that not all of this information goes to our "conscious" minds. It would be too much for us. So we filter out a lot of info. Sometimes our bodies will try to give us information that we didn't know it had if there is an appropriate trigger (like knowing where a lost object is in someone else's house when they are looking for it, even though you did not consciously notice it when it came into your field of vision before.) So, while we cannot prove it yet (no technology to do so), I am willing to bet that our subconscious minds exist partially at a quantum level. This seems obvious if you believe that particles and waves make up the universe and that there is such a thing in the universe as subconsciousness. I believe in this elusive subconscious. It's pretty easy to do, since the general use of the word subconscious seems to refer to practically any function our mind (not to be confused with just the brain, which is one specific location in the body; hardware as opposed to software) carries out that we aren't consciously aware of as it happens.

Since we have minds, and our minds have particles, then the particles in our minds are theoretically capable of communicating with any other particle in the web of connected particles. If our particles have a link, then we do too. Individual particles are only able to communicate very tiny amounts of data, so this link doesn't make us all psychics, but it does indicate that we are all connected—literally, if not meaningfully. That last part is up to us.

I believe all meaning for all minds is invented. Many people long fetishistically for monism. They seem to need to believe that there is an underlying truth to their existence which predates their own lives, which gives them purpose. It's as if they can't trust themselves to allow anything to have new importance, let alone assign that importance based on their own judgment. A self is so complex and multiplicitous, constantly changing and interacting with infinite variables and creatures. It evades definitions and capture habitually, and is impervious to rational deconstruction, which in this age is tantamount to suspicious activity; who would trust a thing like that? (Although having an ally like that could be very useful!) On the other hand, assigning the burden of responsibility to something or someone outside our own selves is just as risky. Allowing other humans to assign meaning to our lives—well, they have these undefinable selves just as we do, and it's generally a pretty safe bet that their selves will be slightly less concerned with ours than their own. What does that leave? Non-humans: gods and abstract ideas and tooth fairies, which are even less certain entities than human minds. Let's not get into how a metaphor for science we don't understand would go about "caring" about individual human lives and experiences long enough to "give" us meanings that are in our best interests, or have anything to do with being living, breathing creatures. So I'm happy to take responsibility for myself. I choose to generate meaning. Existentialism tells us there is no inherent meaning. Nihilists finish the sentence with, "So, what's the point?" I prefer the response of Possibilitarianism, which doesn't exist yet, but could: if there is no limit to the meanings that can be invented and generated and shared, imagine all the possibilities! We can work to create lives that have any meaning we like. What potential.

A poet friend of mine, Victorio Reyes, spoke these words:

> I forget that my life is a poem
> And my world is an ocean
> Of metaphors being drawn
> And redrawn
> To design an epic
> Which is called my life
> Any life

Sadly, if we are going to make our own lives meaningful, there are some problems. For example, how do we know what is real? The only way we experience reality is through our perceptions, which (as we know) are filtered. Whenever I see the word "reality," I immediately replace it in my mind with one of these phrases: shared psychosis, or personal psychosis.

In an experiment about time, electrodes were hooked to peoples' brains to monitor activity. The subjects were measured observing a t-shirt. Then, they were told to close their eyes and remember the shirt. When researchers checked the measurements, they could find absolutely no difference between the brain's responses to seeing the shirt and remembering the shirt. The way the brain behaved was no different at any physical level that we are capable of measuring, yet the subjects themselves were aware of the difference between looking and the memory of looking. This is strange for a number of reasons. Obviously the subjects are getting the information from somewhere, but scientists cannot yet figure out where. We know that once a particle has come in contact with any other particle, they are capable of transmitting information over vast distances and times. I believe that consciousness exists partly at a quantum level, which is why researchers were unable to observe a physical difference between knowing an object physically and knowing it mentally: the awareness was occurring at a level too small to be measured by the devices they were using. Or they weren't looking in the right place. (It could also be the case that both perceptions were equally metaphor, so they look the same in the brain!) Either way, people perceive in unexpected ways that can't all be explained—all our realities are different. At some point, we have to either choose to ignore what we can't explain, or tell ourselves a useful story about it.

Let's take a moment to look at autistic savants. I believe that energy in their brain is being diverted from "normal" areas, which is why the world is so intense for them. Normal sensory data is overwhelming to them, to a degree that renders them generally nonfunctional, yet they all have one instance of heightened perception. They are taking in the same sensory information as the rest of us, but their brains do not interpret it sufficiently, so to them it feels like a garbled mess. The really amazing thing is that they have these very unbelievable talents (hence the word savant). For example: there was one boy who knew the exact second when commercials were beginning and ending on one particular station no matter what time it was, even when there was no radio on for miles around. He had no metal in his mouth (fillings, etc.). We perceive sound in waves, and can interpret it from anywhere between twenty and twenty thousand cycles. Perhaps he was taking information in at a different frequency than most people do, but in the same way. It sounds supernatural, but he just did what we do (only better). All the energy his brain wasn't using "normally" was being used to interpret sound waves at a different range than we do. There are all sorts of autistic savants, but as far as I can tell, all of their talents lie in areas that require the processing of waves and particles in a highly specialized way that seems amazing, but is actually less diversified than what the rest of us do; just incredibly accurate in a more specific range (like instantaneous calculation of the number of pins falling on the ground, etc.). All are examples in which the energy in the brain is being used to interpret different sorts of particles and waves than usual, but it works the same way; they are just tuned to a different frequency. There are other types of mental/physical "illnesses," where different signals are being received (phantom limb, schizophrenia), where the brain transfers these signals in a rash of undecipherable or irrational sensations, or expresses them in a dreamlike way through each person's personal system of symbols.

There are many people who have synaesthesia, where the brain accidentally reads sight as taste, sound as touch, and many other garbled combinations—like a famous composer becoming hypersensitive to the vibrations of sound so that he continued writing music even after he went deaf. So we know that sometimes information that we take in through the body can be confused or not interpreted at all. It can be misinterpreted (when the brain tries to give us information in a way we can understand it, but it doesn't quite make sense to the conscious mind). A classic example of this is paranoid schizophrenia, where sensory information is filtered through the person's terrifying inner symbolism. The processing of sensory data can also be hyper-specified, often at the exclusion of some other functions. Or it could be in the "normal" range.

Perceived reality is the only reality we have access to. Scientists still can't explain all of it, so we can't look to science for a complete personal view of reality. I don't mean to imply that tradition and science have nothing useful to offer. They have many lifetimes' worth of usefulness. Science is wonderful. If we spent our whole life doing calculations to prove that the moon is round, then we would know that, and that would really be something. But we don't have enough time to prove everything ourselves, so we must choose either to trust or to generate a functional mythology. If we do not prove the assumptions ourselves, by the time they get to us, they are stories we read or heard.

It is up to us to create a useful worldview. To do that, we need to figure out what is important to us and behave accordingly. This is where the particle/wave metaphor comes in handy. This universe was made by many fields of potential connecting with each other and becoming real. I think this is a good model for people.

Thinking, creating, learning, and loving: any value-experience we have occurs when the number or quality of the connections we make increases. These are some of the times we remember, the times we base our identities on. We don't just make connections inside our bodies (like new skin growing from old). Obviously we make connections outside them, or we would not be able to connect with sights, sounds, smells, tastes, and touches. So interiority is a funny kind of illusion. Our minds are like bodies without organs, because organs are the tools our bodies grew to make connections, but our minds themselves are connections. (More recent research seems to indicate that our bodies translate information in many more ways than just through the five senses, but that only makes sense, so I won't dwell on it here!)

To steal a metaphor from Gary Zukav: our minds are like a dance. What is a dance? We can write or draw a chart with the steps of a dance, and call it flamenco, but that piece of paper is not flamenco. It is merely a description of flamenco. When a body connects and moves in a certain way: that is flamenco. For that time, that person *is* flamenco: there is no difference between the dancer and the dance. Just like particles and waves. Just like us. There is no difference between the connections we make and ourselves. We are masses of ever-changing connections.

Communicating just means a transfer of energy or information. Every grade school child learns the chain law: if a=b, and b=c, then a=c. But we don't always apply it to our lives. If our bodies are communicating with particles and waves from "outside" of us, and those particles and waves are communicating with those "inside" other people, then in a sense, we are in constant communication with EVERYTHING.

Now for the sad part: remember the story about Columbus? (I first heard about this in the movie *What the Bl**p Do We Know?*) The story goes: When Columbus's boat came over the horizon of the now-American shores, none of the native people could see it, because it did not fit in anywhere with their understanding of the world. Except for the medicine man. He accepted being able to see strange things that no one else could, so it didn't occur to him not to see the boat. He ran around asking people what it was, but nobody else saw anything. So he told them a story in which the thing was just a giant canoe made by the gods, and suddenly they could all see it. Because our brains do not interpret information that makes no sense to us, they do not give it to our conscious minds unless it seems really important. Even our eyesight works that way. We all have blind spots, so our brain fills in the blank spaces in our field of vision with what it expects to be there. Because of what we believe about the "nature" of "reality," we let many boats arrive at our shores without ever seeing or appreciating their potential—or their danger.

To fill in another blind spot, people invented the idea of inherent good and evil. Although these qualities can be projected onto newborns, they don't necessarily have anything to do with the actual child's character. (Falling into absolutism and dichotomy can be dangerous. Infamous "Benjamin" Caplan, a Toronto-based artist, said, "Shirt good. Pants bad." That about sums it up.) Also, "good" and "bad" change value in different societies, so a good person in one may be evil in another, without changing anything other than physical location. Many things are geographically defined. A hub is nothing without spokes. If the effects are not reproducible … you know the rest. No inherent good or evil.

There was once an experiment in which subjects were given a CD player that, unbeknownst to them, had an unusable "song skip" button. Electrodes were placed in their brain, so that whenever an impulse was sent to push the "song skip" button, it was also carried to the CD player, triggering the machine to skip to the next song. Researchers told subjects to look at a clock and announce the time as they decided to push the button. All the subjects were confused because it seemed to them that the machine was skipping to the next song before they decided to push the button! It seemed like the brain sent the command out before the choice was consciously made! They discovered that our consciousness actually experiences a minor lag (like that on live-broadcast television to filter out swear words), so we are never technically conscious in the present moment, and we never hit the future either: we live perpetually in an ever-shifting past. Of course, every moment is another moment's future, and by the same line it's now as well, but in another sense, every moment exists simultaneously. It is always the past until you step outside of time. (Which I pretend can happen when you dream: if our subconscious does exist at a quantum level, and our conscious minds filter its effects, maybe when the conscious mind is turned off, the rules of the subconscious mind apply, and since particles are not bound time-wise ... well. I'm babbling). We have only barely hit the future, and it finds only our naked minds; by the time it is filtered through all of our dressed layers, it is over. Except that it lives again in people's brains, a nearly infinite number of lives, just as we do, and who can say which is more real?

If it were otherwise, (to borrow from George Carlin), we wouldn't have deja-vu, we'd have vuja-de: the feeling that something has never ever happened before! They say deja-vu is just a mistake (a moment goes directly to long- instead of short-term memory), right? But people getting it are a tiny bit closer to perceiving the way the mind really works. They get to feel as if the event happened longer ago than the time they perceived it—which it did. A famous anonymous saying: "Time is the stuff that keeps everything from happening at once." If we did not perceive time linearly, we would go mad. That does not mean time IS linear. In drawing classes, students learn a similar concept. There is no such "thing" as an outline. When we see an outline, it is just an acknowledgement that we aren't perceiving where the "edges" connect to everything else. We must not be tricked into thinking the edge of a model's face is where his existence ends. There is probably a brain and some other stuff tied on to the back of there as well. Of course, that is all conjecture.

When I was a little girl, a professional hypnotist/ magician named Ricky taught me about hypnosis, as well as some simple meditation techniques to expand on what I already knew. One day, I was in my bedroom at home, and I wanted to experiment with partitioning the mind. I had an intense fascination with people who had multiple personalities, and was convinced that it was just an exaggeration of a function already present in "normal" minds.

So I sat on the floor and meditated. I created a mental

space that was to have a different perception of reality than my normal self. I wanted to make it drastically different, so I would know for sure that it had worked. I decided to use sound waves.

I connected with the space in my mind that understood sound waves as physical vibrations instead of the "noise" that our bodies turn them into after interpretation. As a safety, I set up a trigger to snap me out of it: when I saw my cat walk into the room, it would trigger me to return to my everyday awareness.

So, I set up this place in my mind, bundled up all my other beliefs and ideas about the world into a separate location, and then slipped the current, time-bound perceiving self into that room, where it would be cut off from the rest of my "knowledge" about the universe. I meditated there for quite some time.

Then, my mother came into my room and began speaking to me, and the most incredible thing happened.

I heard no sound.

But emitting from her, I saw infinitely complex emanations of waves, ripples, and tides with shimmering particles and patterns and super-positions of states. I watched them travel around the room in awe as they went through some things, reflected off others, and interfered with themselves until they finally dispersed. After some time, my mother became frustrated and left the room, because I wasn't responding ... But how could I? I heard no sound. I only felt and saw it everywhere. My body never translated it into language. I was mesmerized. It was beautiful to watch.

Eventually, my cat came into the room, and the meditation ended. To this day I have no idea what my mother said to me.

I didn't learn much about multiple personalities, but I did learn about personal multiplicities. I think the most incredible thing humans can do is make connections in all of the following ways: learning, thinking, creating, and loving. The entire universe grew out of connections, and as humans, we have the agency to make more of them. Each person helps create the world. Enough people don't take advantage of this power.

In many folk traditions, there is a belief that a strong enough intent or focus on an idea will attract those with similar ideas, or will bring that idea into reality. Obviously we can't create a dragon by wishing hard enough, but if we have intent to find a certain kind of friend or something, because we have given the idea focus and attention, our conscious and subconscious minds will be paying more attention to subtle environmental, temporal, and physical cues that might bring about a meeting. If we devote enough thought to something, we will be more open to perceiving its possibility if we come in contact with it. This is not magic (super-powers) or formulaic science (we could still miss what we are looking for). It is just paying attention.

It is a human habit to project our own spirituality onto something that we don't understand, when there is probably a real scientific explanation that just hasn't been discovered. Then, as soon as it is explained, for some reason, people don't think of it as miraculous, no longer magical...

Luckily, art is still magical.

Meanwhile, I paint, so I hear this question argued about endlessly: What is art? What isn't art? There are many approaches to this issue, but none have ended the debate. The fundamental problem with this question is that it is a fundamentalist question. First people tried to define art according to intent. Then the question of found art arose, and the general consensus seemed to be that if a decision had been made to use it as art, then that was enough intent to make it art. People were so focused on a creator's intentions, they forgot about the importance of observers and interpretations. Most of the arguments that followed had this underlying assumption that for something to be art, someone had to intend for it to be art. This sounds to me like the birth of religion. It is the same as the leap people made when they decided that in order for a universe to exist, someone had to intend a universe to exist. When people went that route, they started questioning whose intent was good enough to call something art and make it stick? Some gods (or artists) made "real" art, and some gods made things that people were tricked into seeing as art. Then, things got really messy. People decided that there could be good art and bad art, and by the time this dichotomy arose, the debate was so distracted from the initial question, everyone just began bickering and making rules and laws about what the art gods really were and how to be one and the whole thing just became a tangled Babel.

The problem with this debate (for me, at least) is that it is based completely on an assumption about a term that is impossible to define, because it is a manner of perspective, which of course makes it a completely individual issue. (Groups of people try to recruit others to their camp, and by sheer mass of supporters they hope to earn the title right. How sinister. I could invent a five-story god who wears red and white winter clothing, but even if I convince millions of people that he exists, that doesn't mean he has any reality outside of the believers' minds. If I slap a toga and some nails on him and call him another god, who knows—the number of total believers could skyrocket. Maybe the idea of him can help their lives in some way, but it doesn't mean you could go visit with him and have tea.)

In my world, the only thermometer for beauty is emotion, whether positive or negative (from intellectual ecstasy to revulsion). So the more deeply something makes you feel, the more beautiful it is to you. Most of us mark our timelines by value experiences, which I consider mostly synonymous with the above definition. I live for those times, to create them in myself and others. I used to write one side of a script in my head, pick a random stranger off the street for coffee, and try to indirectly guide them through the written part of the script without leading them too much. I did not do this to mess with them. I usually tried to bring them around to some useful or interesting conclusion that could help their lives a bit, but beneath it all, I am really just intensely fascinated by how we all work and react. I wanted to learn how to generate specific emotions, specific beauties, and apply that to my art. My life has been filled with a ridiculous amount of serendipitous events, and I adore and anticipate them at every turn. I create because I can't help it. And often, I am lucky enough to revel in the creations of others.

Like life, they leave a convincing impression, which is often so divorced from the mechanics and sleight of hand that we are able to forget that we are also the audience, the observers, and the observed. We are a public creating publics, almost an emergent system—I want to transform the future as well, but I have to pause sometimes and think how funny it is to want to change a thing we cannot help but change.

All the arguments about what art is remind me of a potentially powerful machine: shared reality and shared psychosis. I believe that we can learn a lot from places where things do not function or cease to function. In mathematics, when a complicated problem arises that has infinity in the answer, that is a clue mathematicians use to see where there is something they don't understand. Often, when they go back in and work out whatever the problem was, the answer is no longer infinity. Or it still contains infinity, but they have learned more about the problem, and now have an infinity that brings them one step closer to understanding the problem.

In psychology, we see so many cases where a normal human quality is exaggerated and elaborated to the exclusion of other necessary qualities that allow someone to function in this society. For something to really count as a disorder, it has to negatively impact the person's ability to function in society. Of course, many "psychological disorders" are actually physical ones as well, and some really are so severe that they would cause trouble in any social system. Yet many are only "discovered" when a certain set of traits or qualities are no longer conducive to living in a culture. Some psychological problems are problems of geography. There have been many cultures where some of the people we call schizophrenic would have been shamans.

Those societies had a place for schizophrenia. They used what we call hallucinations as symbolic tapestries that could be used to find a new way of looking at and understanding their world. Because our system does not have a use for them, we call this set of unusual qualities a "disorder." We do not have a place for greedy people who are willing to cause serious long-lasting damage to our planet without remorse. So for the moment that is not a psychological disorder, but perhaps in some other place or time it will be.

Once one of these psychological disorders becomes common, it is de-classified, and lumped back in with the other traits that are considered "normal" ways of being human. A friend's psychologist told him there is no such thing as one Attention Deficit Disorder. Each person's is completely unique. Does that sound like a specific disease, or a set of qualities that make it difficult to function efficiently in this particular society? Almost everyone I meet has been diagnosed with ADD, or could be. And I know some really amazing people. Being lucky enough to know all these amazing people, I noticed something strange. None of them had any trouble focusing, if they were in environments they were comfortable with, doing things they cared about. They only had trouble with attention when they had to do things that didn't seem important to them. It is only the requirements of the particular societies they are living in that make it difficult for them to function "normally." If they were able to live in a place that did not require anything of them—except that they pursue their thirst for learning, creation, and living—they would not have a disorder at all. They would be in order. When people are given medicine for this, they are not given medicine to fix their selves. They are given medicine to fix the way their selves function in society. I don't mean to imply that people who actually have ADD don't sometimes need help to get along in this culture. I am making a distinction. Some "disorders" are descriptions of serious problems that individuals would have no matter where or when they live. (I think that this kind of disorder will eventually be understood as a physical problem). Other "disorders" are descriptions of the problems in the relationships between specific individuals and their society. Psychology does not yet seem to separate these.

Art faces a similar problem. It is a relative description. There needs to be room for it to be different things to individuals and cultures. To one country, Picasso's "Guernica" is art. To someone who lives in the desert and needs to build shelter, it might not be. It might be fabric for a tent. As a relative idea, "art" is anywhere you see it. Anything can be art if someone gives it permission.

We all know about shared psychosis. We see it every day: in the wars between people and the wars within ourselves. Many of us learn to hide our inner worlds to avoid social punishment. I saw a performer called Thor in a park in New York who had made an art out of living the way he wanted to. He dressed strangely, and skillfully played a violin while singing in many voices—often in nonsense words he made up himself. I thought it was beautiful. There was a captivating aesthetic style that was fascinating and consistent in everything he created, and it inspired me to try to be braver about sharing my inner world through my art, in hopes of catalyzing others to do the same. A huge crowd gathered and watched this man in fascination, but most of them seemed embarrassed to be looking. They were uncomfortably interested, and from the comments I overheard as they whispered to each other, they were watching this brave artist like a specimen that escaped his freak-container. When the performance ended, and he spoke intelligently and articulately to the audience, many of them startled involuntarily. It was okay to watch this poor outsider behave strangely in public, but to be forced to recognize that he was as intelligent (if not more so) as they were was almost too much for them to understand. Maybe these people don't have strong inner worlds, and all I was witnessing was surprise. I doubt that very much. The chances of growing up human without developing any internal symbolism or quirkiness are very small. Many people get so used to suppressing the most unique aspects of themselves that just to get by they forget and become their own delusion. We can't help but do this to some degree. I watched as his very presence challenged what they believed about their own choices in life.

I'm sure some of them chose to forget the impact of his display and went on about their regular lives, but I'm also willing to bet that a lot of people remembered what they had witnessed: it is possible to express yourself. It is possible to let people see reflections of your inner world, to live your art, to not be horribly punished for it. It is possible that some people might find it beautiful and be moved to create more beauty. And if we're very lucky, it is possible we'll get to see it.

In *Darkness Moves*, Henri Michaux wrote that, "One needs unbelievable willpower to pull off a face, so accustomed is it to its man." When I paint, by allowing subconscious imagery to interact with logical systems, I attempt to access interstitial zones where new meanings can be generated and transferred by a gust of whim. The inner worlds I paint are love letters to strangers' subconscious selves. I want to lure them away from their faces.

Relationships (with our multiplicity of selves, with friends, with lovers, with everything) can be like that performer from the park. Any connection has the potential to be art. Every time we make a connection, we are creating a new zone of possibilities. We can choose to hide ourselves and hope things somehow will be okay (and sometimes they are just that: okay). Or, we can seize the opportunity to let ourselves be intrigued by the mystery of otherness, and let our inner worlds emerge and inform each other to create new worlds together. If meaning is generated, we can allow these interstitial zones to be as important as we dare. If we are very brave, we can allow our connections with others to move us, so they, and we, and all of the worlds we inhabit breathe art.

"I am your distress, the seam in the wall that opens to the wind and its stammering ... and how I might acquit you of this hiddenness, and prove to you that I am no longer alone, that I am not even near myself anymore." — Paul Auster

Humans are such powerful and fragile creatures. When you hold a heart in your hand (your own or someone else's), the responsibility is immense. But there is nothing like the feel of its warm rhythm as it pulses and stains and seeps into your skin, and sings to your mythic veins that they don't have to be alone. We grow so used to independence. It is a terrifying thing to love. Everything is at risk, and that risk wakes you up, reminds you what art is and what it means to be alive. It reminds you of your power to create. It is scary being an artist, even scarier to be human, and it's even more terrifying to be both. To be a man or woman means that we have the power to create. What responsibility. What possibilities. I believe it is worth the risk.

Peace King

Papi Kymone Freeman

D ax—steel sharpens steel. Glad you are on the job. The
work you are doing is invaluable by documenting our
lives. Before our lives are over, we got to do an anthology
on the resurgence of the Black Arts Movement like Larry Neal/
Amiri Baraka did with *Black Fire*.

But that is after we have done some big shit!

Believe/belief? Whoa …

Are you familiar with the anti-drug campaign in
Baltimore called BELIEVE? It is everywhere. Str8 bullshit too,
since B-More has the highest concentration of heroin addicts in
this country. Not to mention that *The Wire* ain't make "believe."

Anyway, I have the festival, my first short film, another
production of the play, a self-destruction remake to finish, a baby
on the way, and a weed habit to attend to, so I must be brief
here.

The first think that came to mind upon pondering this is

the story of my grandfather's funeral. He passed away from cancer on Juneteenth. At his funeral I was finally officially recognized as the "artist" in the family, even though I was ridiculed and discouraged throughout my life for "believing" I could be. So they asked me to read a poem at Big Pop's final day.

I read Langston Hughes's "A Negro Speaks of Rivers," very slowly. Then I said a few words.

When I was three years old, my grandfather taught me how to swim by throwing me into twelve feet of water and told me to keep kicking. Though shocking, this didn't strike me as very profound until after someone asked me later did he "really" do that, because they couldn't swim and if they were in that situation they would have drowned.

I realized right then and there that it is all about belief. A three-year-old doesn't believe it can't swim. It only believes it doesn't know how to swim. So with the right encouragement (en courage) it will struggle to do its very best by continuing to kick and learning how to stay afloat.

However, a thirty-year-old, though more physically capable, believes he can't swim and will quickly give up—be overcome by fear, and only learn how to drown.

What we believe decides who we are, what we can do and where we are willing to go.

Like: Do you believe in creation or evolution? I submit that once it was a fact that all human life originated in Afrika; the Eurocentric world invented Darwinism, claiming that man evolved from monkeys, therefore making black people the closest link to apes and white people the highest form of human development.

If you believe that, I can sell you land on the moon (which will be available for purchase soon, albeit not through me). How could this possibly be when there is no other instance in nature of a select few within a species evolves and the others remain the same?

Darwinist theory should be dispelled by the mere

continued existence of apes. I believe that it is the cornerstone of white supremacy right behind the belief Christopher Columbus "discovered" a land already occupied.

Hope this helps ...

PS—my grandfather's name was John M. Richardson (6/27/30—6/19/07)

"We are the stories we are told. They create boundaries in our voices."— Haki R. Madhubuti

BUZZER

Start Over.

By Mark Gorney

The other day I read about rabbits taking over Robben Island, South Africa, the site of Nelson Mandela's long incarceration. Authorities announced that a cull of the rabbits will be followed by "a sterilisation programme aimed at allowing a small and manageable population of rabbits." Can we have a small and manageable population of humans?

Patient (Earth) is ill. Diagnosis: Excess of Homo Sapiens, carbon, pollution, and iniquity, disruption of balance/natural law.

Life on Earth is bizarre, surreal, beautiful, and insane. Humans are as inexplicable a presence on this planet as ferns, dinosaurs, mastodons, ice ages, or pikas. We have two legs, opposing thumbs, sometimes a brain and the tendency to breed like rabbits and run rampant all over the globe. At least rabbits

113

are kept in check by foxes, coyotes, lynxes, eagles, hawks, and what not. At this point humans aren't kept in check by anything. At least not yet.

If the history of Earth was condensed into 365 days, humans appeared somewhere around the last second of New Year's Eve. So in the scheme of millennia, human civilization is but a blip—a flash in the pan. From that perspective, does what happens in this particular phase of Earth's history really matter? Perhaps not, but in the here and now I believe this blip didn't really flash "correctly." Here are some idealistic, impossible, and probably altogether ludicrous ways of re-imagining this blip.

Pope said, "The proper study of mankind is man." But if you feel that the proper study of mankind is Earth—that Earth is the subject, the focal point—then you might observe that at this blip in time, this planet, the "patient," is ill. Our aging planet has a disease, or at least a fever. We've infected the planet by being here, to say nothing of the extreme cruelty we've shown one another in the process.

Humans are the first life form to break free, as it were, at least temporarily from some of the laws of nature. We are the first to affect the planet itself, yet we are a product of this planet. Or are we? We are "natural." Or are we? Wherever we came from, we are bacteria that are creating Koyaanisqatsi— life out of balance. We are disrupting Earth's natural cooling system, altering the temperature, creating drought and storms, and poisoning it (and ourselves).

Why this is happening and why the planet has "allowed" it to happen are unknown to me. Who knows how long we will continue to get away with it before nature really does something about it? The planet should not "mind" having us here; we should not throw the planet out of balance, nor should we really have much of an impact on it. I would have thought this was a gibbon (I mean given), but apparently not. We're devouring our host. When we will be thrown off or out?

Unlike other life forms, our population is currently

seemingly unregulated. We're spreading all over the place. We used to not exist, then there were about 100,000 of us, then a million, then a billion, and now about 6.7 billion, all within about the last 100,00 years. And it's predicted that there will be nine billion of us before our numbers finally start to decline. To me, nine billion is a terrifying number; even 6.7 billion is too many.

Non-human life forms simply perish when their numbers are excessive, and the environment is unaffected. But humans just keep on going—stomping, eating, or melting everything in their way. It would be one thing if humans were carbon-neutral and the planet was pristine, but we're not and it's not. We're trashing it with our carbon and other gaseous activities, which include bovine flatulence. Homo Flatus Erectus.

To my idealized and/or naïve way of thinking, I view the manner in which human beings have proliferated and flourished on this planet as being some sort of bacteria-like "mistake" and a deviation from what could/might have been instead: a planet with a limited civilization, a sort of "best of," with minimal impact on the planet.

Can't we take the take the best of man's ingenuity (sanitation, aqueducts, electricity, refrigeration, the Internet) and have them co-exist with fecund, undisturbed forests and vast, pristine wetlands?

I desire perfectly functioning pristineness (even if that's not a word). I want crystal clear water, healthy coral reefs exploding with color, bountiful schools of colorful fish, all manner of outrageous marine life, and the Amazon and the polar ice caps in their totality. I want gorillas, bison, and manatees. I want an unmolested ecosystem. I'll say it again. I want an unmolested ecosystem. And the Internet. Is it possible to have both?

I know this is impossible idealism at its either finest or worst, but my elusive dream is of another world: Venice, Amsterdam, and water-based civilizations, coastal and tropical cities and towns as they were from the 19th century up until the 1950s/60s (of course free from squalor or socio-economic iniquity), a few New Yorks or Londons, architectural intelligence and splendor, peaceful labor, trade, cooperation, creativity, competition and evolution, canals, trains, trams, funiculars, bicycles, ships, boats, ferries, and the odd monorail.

So where would these idealized humans live, how many of them should there be, and what would they do? Well, much the same as what they do currently, just about six billion less of them.

If we came from Tanzania, can someone tell me how in tarmigration we wound up in Siberia or Greenland? If, for some genetic reason not understood by me, you were migrating and upon reaching a place where it got really cold at night at certain times of the year, wouldn't you head back? Yes there goes skiing, frolicking in the snow, and *The Shining*, but let's look at how we are made: we have skin, not fur. In my view humans belong in relatively warm places, but not in the middle of the desert. That's for lizards.

There is certainly room for people on this planet, but can we skip the manifest destiny that cleared Europe of its woodlands, including primeval forests[1], Brazil of swaths of the Amazon, or the US of most of its ecosystem? Native Americans, while then living in a fashion that that would be hard for a lot of us now, at least lived life in harmony with nature. From the perspective of the natural world, the US was much better off before the arrival the true savages: Europeans.

Is it not possible for some millions of us to reside in places where it's warm, where there are a lot of nice beaches, and where we are close to and can get around on water? For the most part humans are to wildlife as WD40 is to moisture, but if you're going to have people, put a select number of them along the coasts and riverine regions of Greece, Italy, Spain, Sicily, Capri, Sardinia, Malta, Crete, Algeria, Morocco, Zanzibar,

----

[1] *Heavenly Caves: Reflections on the Garden Grotto*, Naomi Miller, 1982.

Palestine, Jerusalem, Lebanon, or even Australia, Thailand, Bali, or Vietnam. After the day's work is done, food, drink, music, discussion, and democracy at a café by the water's edge, on the beach under the stars, on a ferry, boat, or gondola, by the fountain(s) in the main piazza/square, on an ancient bridge or among crumbling ruins or in a cool underground water cavern/cistern such as the capacious Roman example in Istanbul, complete with tall arches and support columns, tasteful illumination and some fish in the massive floor of water.

I guess I inherited my mother's dislike of being far from a large body of water—plus humans are about sixty percent water by weight. Oceans, lakes, and rivers are endless sources of wonder and a source of food: fish and crustaceans. And provided you're not in a storm or squall, I find transportation by water to be quite pleasant, soothing, and logical. That is a good part of my fascination with "water" cities like Venice and Amsterdam. Even though the former is sinking and becoming a touristy museum void of actual working residents, I love it as a semi-pinnacle of civilization. The incredible, beautiful, perfect architecture, the canals coursing through the city like blood through a body, and the fact that you can get anywhere via the canals. The only thing is that they're filthy. So clean them up and you've got it made? Amsterdam—the same only cleaner. In these and other cities, canal boats, trams, bicycles, and walking would be the dominant modes of transport. (More) houses could be built over water, so you can drive your boat into your home, go up into it and at night be lulled to sleep by the sound of lapping water.

Lakes are lovely, and rivers—essential parts of human culture—are arteries. Grottoes are literally cool and are a part of our civilized past[2]. You could have giant restaurants or other places of entertainment, where you dine on boats in the middle

----
[2] Chapter 1, "A Lingering Scent of Eden," *The World Without Us*, Alan Weisman, 2007.

of a huge, natural or man-made grotto with a Tiki bar in the middle. Flaming torches and music. The following (taken from a "review" I wrote) is what would lurk at the bottom of a fictitious neighborhood place called The Grotto:

> (An) underground cave with world-class stalactites and stalagmites and extensive navigable rivers and lakes illuminated by tasteful underwater lighting. Get in one of the free paddle or rowboats and drift along in cool silence punctuated only by the occasional flutter of bats, drips of water, and the quiet murmuring of the few other boaters. All of the rivers lead to another world, as yet unexplored.

Architecture, building materials, design, and locations all have a profound affect on people. Whereas I am energized and inspired by old buildings, there is certainly room for new building styles and technologies, as long as they are intelligently designed and implemented. Think about what you're building, where it goes, how it's integrated into the environment and the light inside.

You can make a palace or prison. The incredible Frank Lloyd Wright-designed Marin Civic Center is an outrageously Buddhist-retro-modern sort of administrative temple that houses, among other entities, the Courts and other aspects of the penal justice system. But its inspired, cathartic, natural-light-filled open spaces, paint colors, greenery, and ubiquitous golden globes are healing—as if to say to the wayward, the angry, or the unenlightened who might pass through the premises: "This is the way—not violence." Trees, streams, and creeks in and through buildings create good feng shui.

Every city, town, and village should be as "perfect" as it can be in terms of population size, architecture, and economic activity. Can't people and/or the wise philosopher kings or the Council of Elders be trusted to work out a compromised solution that results in something acceptable?

My romanticized vision is inspired in part by turn-of-the-century postcards of just about any city or town along the

Mediterranean, the coasts of Africa, the Middle East, or the Caribbean. I know full well that colonialism was in full sway at this time and even if the country was not colonized, what's on the postcard was the charming downtown or an important building, never the slums. It's just that the nice parts of these places, at least from an architectural standpoint, were so cool. The goal is to have a pleasing and practical aesthetic along with the promise of a level of modernity and a decent life for everyone. We can't all have an enormous house and I don't see that Ferraris (or cars for that matter) are necessary, but it would be nice to see the coexistence of prosperity and everyone at least having the basic necessities.

Very big cities, which might be necessary as powerhouses of thought and progress, can work if designed intelligently, with quality of life in mind. Is New York an example of this? Although it's freezing in the winter, possibly, but mega-cities like these cannot exist at the expense of its residents or the environment.

On the walls of my kitchen I have two framed maps of San Francisco—one from 1846-47, the other from 1915. The pre-gold rush map has a grand total of thirty houses, all near the beach, with tons of space in between. Sleepy, provincial, and well integrated into nature, you could probably hear the lapping of the water near what is now Portsmouth Square in Chinatown. The 1915 map is much closer to how the city is now, although still appealing to me on account of the architecture. It's built-up and bustling, with landfill, wharves, freight trains, and heavy industry. (I believe in rail transport, and have an obsession with San Francisco's old freight railroads. Despite the fact that they were powered by coal, they carried much greater loads than trucks, so were actually greener in the long run. And modern railroads are infinitely greener than today's trucks.)

What I am proposing is some sort of in-between: as judicious an amalgam as possible. People need jobs, food, supplies, economic activity, and a standard of living, but we need put be intelligent about where we put and how we handle the manufacture of all the things we both need and want.

Except where some necessary natural resource exists, the interior of continents could be off limits to humans. How about only populating, say, ten-percent of the globe? With the exception of a few limited HPAs (Human Population Areas) on the coasts of California and Central and South America, the entire western hemisphere could be people-free.

One thing I have not worked out (as if I have the rest of it figured out) is ZPG vs. the natural tendency of population to increase (inability to withdraw penis before ejaculation or use of birth control). This is a problem. It is the tendency of the Universe to want more and more. The urges to have intercourse, ejaculate into the vagina, and breed are often irresistible. In order to attain ZPG, a necessary requirement for this world, humans will have to make sacrifices. If censuses find that population is increasing, there would have to be either voluntarism or financial incentives to control population growth.

Inspired by the Jamaican original "Birth Control," the Specials asked, "Do you really want a programme of sterilisation?" People should show some "self control" (ha). And it they don't, offer tax incentives to those that don't breed. I don't have an answer to this problem, but we'll need some sort of volunteer or imposed regulatory mechanism in this regard. My father thought something should be put in the water supply that would result in sterility. That may be a bit extreme, but the motto of the Voluntary Human Extinction Movement[3] is "May we live long and die out." A scenario that assumed that all fertile women are henceforth limited to one child would result in a population of just 1.6 billion by the year 2100.

I believe in intelligent government and/or rule of philosopher kings, but I also believe in human creativity and initiative. If you want to start a 78 rpm record label or become

----

[3] VHEMT website: http://www.vhemt.org

a taxidermist of giant swordfish, go for it. There will always be iniquity in that all humans are not created equally. While some have bigger brains than others, we will always need street sweepers. But there's no reason that that street sweeper can't stop sweeping for a few minutes to tell you what he thinks of Plato or Nietzsche or Adorno or Asmahan, Homayra or Rosa Eskenazi, or how he wishes the city would buy those gasoline-powered sweepers that you drive.

As if it needs to be pointed out, there's no need or excuse for war, slavery, torture, genocide, famine, starvation, oppression, discrimination, or extreme poverty. Especially in a smaller population size, there is enough to go round for everyone, provided people are intelligent, motivated, and free of greed. And I know that's a lot to ask for. I believe in progress, but how about progress without war, slavery, or colonialism? Development without exploitation? I know, I am assuming humans are fundamentally different than they are.

I'd like to think we're "evolving," but I'm not so sure. Are we really making progress? In some ways, yes—it's just that there are too many of us, and the degree to which we are raping, devouring, and trashing the planet and encroaching on, endangering, and eliminating multitudes of plant and animal species[4] is appalling. It's a holocaust.

Let elephants and gorillas roam without fear of being shot. Personally I have no problem with eating fish or chicken, but don't hack the fins off sharks and throw them back in the sea to die. Stop slaughtering whales, seals, dolphins, and turtles, and please cease eating chimps, monkeys, dogs, and cats. The mind reels.

I am obsessed with the idea of a healthy, balanced planet and a limited number of humans co-existing with all manner of flora and fauna now, in their totality, as they were before the

----

[4] Endangered species list: http://www.earthsendangered.com/list.asp

"advent" of people. I saw an online comment somewhere that Earth needs a "reset." I couldn't agree more.

I've started to share some of these ideas with friends. One challenged me by offering the thought that civilization might have to be a bit messy, we may have to make some sort of an impact on the planet if we want to progress, smaller cities and towns are not conducive to the great strides in civilization brought about by great metropolises like New York or London, and that perhaps it will someday be possible to manipulate and/or tame nature. Could be. And I am torn in the respect that the great cities of the world have aspects that are truly great. Can we keep those, yet stay out of nature's way?

For now, though, I walk along Canal Cinq with a new novel I heard about called Jamaica. The story is that hundreds of years ago "British" people stole "Africans," packed them into "slave" ships and sent them thousands of miles across the ocean to a small "colony" island in the "Caribbean" called "Jamaica." The "slavemasters" forced the slaves to work from sunup until sundown in unimaginably brutal conditions on plantations harvesting "sugar cane" so the British could sweeten their tea(!). Well eventually Jamaica was given independence from "Britain," and some descendants of the slaves, now poor people living in "ghettoes" of the capital, Kingston, created a protest music called "reggae," whose chief exponent was a brilliant, mixed-race rebel/poet/rabble-rouser musician named Bob Marley, who died relatively young of a disease called "cancer." He describes how the music came about and how popular it became all over the world. It's quite a story.

I also picked up the latest edition of the ever-popular illustrated magazine *The Rest of the World*. The lead article is about flamingoes. They turned up in a weird dream I had the other night after eating too many sardines. There was this pale, pasty guy in white shorts, white socks, and a straw hat with a red, white, and blue flag pin who waddled out of his generic white house and bent down with some effort to pick up some newsprint that had nothing printed on it. For some reason in front of his house there was about an acre of perfectly manicured green grass being watered automatically by some sort of device that sprayed water around. On the grass were a bunch of plastic flamingoes. I don't know what it meant.

Postscript 1: One of the many uncertainties I have about my modest "proposal" was further clarified the other day by a magazine ad I saw touting the pristineness (why isn't this a word) of Oregon's coasts and the fact that the entire coast is public land. As they say in Kazakhstan, "Niiiice!"

Postscript 2: I believe in goats. And lizards.

www.worldisc.net

A Lesson in Humbleness

Erin Turner

From the time children are born we wonder, "What will they be when they grow up?" In fact that question, "What will you be?" will be asked of that child for most of his or her young life. And while it's a perfectly encouraging and innocent question—after all we are all going to be something—it's interesting how our jobs, our career, our success is such a defining reflection of who we are as a person.

From as early as I can remember, I was double- and triple-checking my homework so that I could turn it in "perfect" and receive the recognition I so eagerly awaited. As I became a bit older, I also became a bit less anal retentive, but I never was able to shake the need for success, or that ever-important career, so that I could someday proudly earn that title, whatever it might be, when I finally grew up.

When I hit high school and I began to focus, by college I was driven. I think the fact that my parents didn't have much money drove me even harder. I knew I didn't want to scrape by in my adult life, but I also knew that if there was something I wanted (a car, an apartment, clothes), I had to earn it myself. So by the time I was twenty, I was paying my full tuition in college, working to pay for my apartment and books, and working two internships ... inching me closer.

After graduating with a degree in broadcast journalism, I FINALLY could get what I was seeking since as long as I could remember! So I hopped from small town to small town, climbing my way to bigger titles in better markets. Meanwhile I was earning little money and therefore continued to work a second job just to scrape by ... but I had the title! Yet as hard as I worked, I never felt like I had achieved anything. Perhaps it was because all the happiness and satisfaction I thought the jobs and titles and "air-time" I received really didn't matter at the end of the day when I went home to my lonely apartment in the middle of nowhere. I had everything that I had set out to accomplish, yet I had never felt so empty. I'm grateful for those nights of solitude for allowing me to see that what I was desperately in search of wasn't what I needed at all.

Although I realized several years ago the need to let go of my ego, and therefore leave the job I clawed my way to get, recently I've been reminded about the need for faith in some sort of a plan, and how important "letting go" is in order to get anywhere. Although I'm no longer chasing that news carrot, I still find myself questioning who I am and what I will become. As the mythological story of Gilgamesh states, what you fear all along (not earning that title) is usually what you end up facing, as I am right now in my adult life. But while I'm in a state of transition in my career, I am consciously, and maybe even subconsciously trying not to let my changing titles define who I am, and instead allow myself to find my next path without force or struggle by opening myself up to what is presented.

So while I can tell my father has a hard time accepting that he can't brag about his daughter "the television reporter," and I hear him always inquiring about what I'm doing with my day, what he doesn't know and what I don't feel obligated to explain is that I have never been happier in my life. Isn't that what we all really want? Shouldn't that be enough of an accomplishment? And although I am writing and producing more than I ever expected to as a new mom, I often don't tell him about the work I do so that he can, as I have, accept me for who I am, not what role defines me. Humble: that's the next title I'm working towards.

www.citystretch.com

The Playhouse

Erica DeLorenzo

When I was growing up, we had a one-room playhouse in our backyard that we used mostly for playing games or storing outdoor toys. It was big enough for a few kids, had windows with bright yellow trim to match the door, and was conveniently close to the tire swing. Then sometime around third or fourth grade, with no rhyme or reason that I can remember, the playhouse started to evolve into a personal refuge. I spent hours and hours decorating it and filling it with books, dragging blankets from the house so I could stay out there even when the weather turned cold. My own bedroom became quite insufficient—perhaps because I had realized that the rules of my parents governed that space, while the playhouse escaped their attention. From the playhouse-sized rafters, I hung crystals and pictures and things I had collected in the "woods," like feathers and stones, and I would race home from school to read or draw or think in my new nest. Never quite at home in a world or family that rarely allowed time for reflection and quiet, I needed a place where I could try to make sense of the life that I was beginning to understand I had.

One day, as I was daydreaming, I started to imagine the playhouse into some sort of time-space vehicle that had transported me here from a very different place. I actually began to fantasize about where "I" really came from, and invented a game that I hoped would make everything clear. I would stand in the middle of the playhouse and spin around and around and around until I got dizzy and, in what must have seemed quite bizarre to my parents or neighbors, burst open the door hoping to have arrived somewhere much more familiar. I was always disappointed that it was the same old backyard.

For a long time, whenever I thought back on that time in my life, I thought I was just a weird kid who eventually stopped going to the playhouse when she got caught up in navigating the social strata of middle and then high school. Though I never outgrew that introverted and contemplative part of myself, it was a very long time before I knew it was okay to think outside the proverbial box (or remembered why it was important to do so). I don't know where I got the past-life or mystical ideas, but it was not an approved topic of conversation in my house or with anyone in my extended family. As a result, I spent many, many years struggling between conforming and rebelling before I was finally comfortable in my own skin and in my own way of experiencing this time and place.

For me the playhouse is a metaphor for my own mind— the place that I need to be quiet and still but at the same time, a safe haven to explore thoughts and ideas about mySelf. Obviously, as many times as I dizzyingly burst open the front door of that playhouse, the world and my reality never physically changed. What I didn't know then, but what I learned later on, was that the right questions and answers about my life, and the power to change my experience of that reality, resided in what was happening in the playhouse. That a ten-year old can know, on some basic human level, that there is a need to sit and contemplate in stillness, must say something about the value of meditation.

As with the many stories that make up my life, in the larger context this one is not just about my journey, but about the personal journey, which I believe to be cyclical and repetitive in nature, not linear. Over and over again, through this life and others, we have the opportunity (some of us a natural inclination or even determination) to go to the "playhouse" and remember who we are, what we are doing here, and where we are going. You can expand this framework across multiple lifetimes, apply it directly to this particular existence, or use it in relation to each and every present moment. In any case, the recurring theme of mindfulness is always the same and is always powerful.

The playhouse in the backyard is long gone, but that doesn't really matter. I have realized the more important thing is that I can go to the figurative playhouse anytime, and that I should not need the physical structure or even optimum circumstances to practice meditation. The objective is to continually find that place of stillness and truth in everything we do, no matter what is swirling around us, and to believe that we are exactly where we should be.

Change is Truth

Nat Rahav

In the world there are many illusions.
One particularly clever one is belief.

Beliefs change. Truth is eternal.
Belief in Truth is also an illusion.

Beliefs Change.
Truth is Eternal.
Change is Truth.

www.busquelo.org

What Do I Believe?
(Stream of Konsciousness)

Sensei Marc Coronel, B.A.

D o you put your faith in God? Do you bless the ones still breathing? Do you believe if you live good you will go to heaven, be reincarnated, see your loved ones? So many questions, not enough days. I live in the now and borrow from the past to avoid the future. Where do I start? Should I theorize about God, Allah, Abba, Shiva, Buddha, Krishna, or some guy who tells me that the aliens are coming soon and Tom Cruise is my example of exemplary living?

what do you believe?

I think I will live in the now,
not wondering about the when, where or how.
I love life and what it has given me,
feelings to cherish, thoughts to relish and people who are
"free."

Born in a house with: Jesus on the wall,
Buddha on the floor down the hall,
A Bible sitting atop the Torah,
Shiva in the window, next to a bronze menorah.
Mahabharata on the TV,
The Last Emperor now on DVD.

My family is so diverse,
I look at this more like a blessing than a curse.
Mixed like a fine track where the needle of life does not discern
if I like salsa or hip hop.
I love being what I am, not pure and undiluted, not the cream
but the crop.

I believe that if you live your life to the fullest, you can indulge
and enjoy everything life has to offer without hurting anyone.

My life has been a roller coaster of belief, and I have seen my
people head to different cults, groups, or belief systems, and
follow a self proclaimed Guru to live like a nomad, while the
Guru is rolling around in an S-Class Mercedes. Most of the
people that "guide" us to where we are lead a more backward
life than we think. Divorce, adultery, lying, cheating: all made
possible because they possess knowledge that people are looking
for. All you have to do is ask someone who is grounded in your

opinion or read a book! These days they have such books on audiotape, or even better, downloadable! I don't believe in what the gurus try to "sell," but I am amazed at what they are capable of doing with their bodies, since there is a connection between body and mind. The tracks are laid for the train of consciousness, but the disturbance in balance within the bodies of people who have no equilibrium in their personal lives will greatly affect the performance of their consciousness and the way their message is conveyed to the masses. They come in all forms, and the more powerful they are, the more commotion they can stir up, knowing that there will be a "please follow me" mentality. I follow my heart and have the understanding that my values for the last thirty years will keep me on the straight but not narrow, since there cannot be growth if you have your eyes looking in only one direction. Growth comes from enlightenment; it comes from allowing people to shed light unto your life and into your life.

Light comes in different forms, knowledge, experiences, feelings, and human beings.

A Being is out there for all of us,
An Entity who reflects our opposite thoughts in difference.
In Insolence do we live life without a fuss?
But Normalcy forces us to give deference,
To Genius in disguise,

Who Will I meet prior to my demise?
Will I be remembered through children's eyes?
Or Cloaked, robed, and put on a wall.
For Knowing enough of the kids in the hall,
Who's Entire existence depends on us all.
Not Dreaming anymore is our biggest flaw.

what do you believe?

Today I sit at a lake while hearing children swim, play, and being
pulled around on inner tubes by parents. How fun life could be?
Our children are watching a comedian share his funny stories
about a sad life in a hilarious way; that's what I deem to be
brave. Yesterday Gary, Dedra, Jian, Mace, and I went to see the
Boston Red Sox spank the Baltimore Orioles, as a rookie pitcher
in his second game pitched a no-hitter in Fenway Park. This
was Mace's first major league game (at three years old), made
possible through Gracie's childhood friends Becky and Gary. An
experience that is in stone through the ages. Our son has no
clue he was a part of history, in what I believe could he be a
significant part of the future. His first major league game; he
likes baseball, god knows how since it is nowhere in our house.
We have beautiful seats, Mace is having a great time, he expects
this to be a short visit to a park where everybody screams at
field with baseball players on it. They showed his face on the
big screen. It was a magical game. During the 7th inning stretch,
he received a bag of Cracker Jacks. Before the game we bought
him the jersey of the player who saved the game from being just
another ordinary baseball game by diving for a grounder and
gassing it to first for the out. When the pitcher finished the game,
Mace managed to be the only person watching to be carried on
to the field by a hostess in celebration. Now what if I believe in
signs and omens? Will my son be a great baseball player or a
person of distinction who is looked at (already) by people to be
an enigma? I believe that to be true. I just hope he can show the
wicked, who prey on intelligence that his knowledge is beyond
their grasp. I pray for all my children that they will always see
the world as an ever-changing globule and adapt accordingly. I
already see that in Gooch and Wyntergrace as well. Mace is just
the enigma in our life, and I am interested to see how his life will
unfold, and how we, his loving family, will affect his behavior and
development. I love being a father and a role model; I make a

lot of mistakes and try to be as open as possible to my family as they point my faults out to me, which is a hard thing to do. I try to grow from each mistake and not repeat it.

September 14, 2007

I believe life is love, happiness, health, and karma.
Put it in the air and it will be created as belief.
Be it in joy or in grief.
My thoughts are here in confusion...
What I believe is becoming a delusion.

I'm looking for a specific answer, but my life takes its turns on the daily, so maybe I can keep an eye on the proverbial ball to keep it all order.

For everyone looking to see what they believe, please don't look, just live a life that won't harm anyone, yourself included. I don't think in this world of belief that there is one person who can tell us how to live; there is no solution. Don't always do unto others as was done on to you. Don't always pass the ball exactly the way it came. Oh please don't be one of those people...

Always think good and do good, as good is what society expects you to do. Just keep in sight what you "believe" or feel to be just and righteous. If you exude what you feel than you can believe what you live.

www.openmindfitness.com

Quantam Physics and Me

Caroline Leavitt

O kay, the first thing you have to know is that I'm not crazy. My husband's an atheist (though I insist he just hasn't seen the quantum physics light of things), but I believe in psychics, ghosts, astrology, mediums, shamans, reincarnation, and, yep, God, though certainly not the white-haired old white guy who sits on a cloud and meddles in everyone's lives. My God's more of a force in the universe. If you aren't about to make fun of me yet, let me add that I also believe all of the above has a scientific track it runs on—quantum physics.

Quantum physics is so compellingly strange, so weird and inspiring, that I think there surely must be an explanation for all of life, a theory of everything that comforts, consoles, and also makes perfect sense. Everything is energy, there is no time, so why shouldn't a psychic be able to snatch onto some of that and tell the future? Why shouldn't that energy appear as a ghost? If time is a loop, why shouldn't we always be as alive as we are dead? Energy healing is simply being able to manipulate the energy in the body to allow the body to heal itself. Tarot cards work with archetypes that even Carl Jung approved of. (Trust me, they work.)

To me, the universe is this wide open, immensely exciting and strange place where anything is possible except a God who sits on a throne and judges people, or a hell with snarling demons and pitchforks. That's even too far-fetched for the likes of me to believe. But science is my own personal religion, my door to all of the so-called farfetched things that people don't understand yet, and the more I study physics, the more I see the incredible mystery and magic of things.

There's a great Chinese proverb: "Don't say 'This is impossible' to the person who is busy doing it." And that goes for immersing yourself in new notions of God, reincarnation, telepathy, tarot, and my new personal favorite, parallel universes.

www.carolineleavitt.com

I believe that music is the universal language. Music transcends race, religion, and politics. Music's ability to communicate and heal the soul, as well as the body, shows us this fact constantly. Music is in everything, the vibrations that hold atoms in harmony, to the song that the winds and oceans create as they move in harmony with mother earth.

Peace,
Maurice Oliver/Chill Factor-5
Electronfarm Records

To Believe Is to Have Libido or Love For
Etymological Play Honoring a Root Metaphor of Living

William G. Doty

C omfortable with the editor's decision not to focus this collection upon belief in or about, I explore some of the ways in which the various cognates of "belief" may lead to one thread that the etymologies of these words repeatedly enfold: libido/love for. Not necessarily for another person, or an object we might aim at on Earth Day, but I'll suggest, a more aim-less, non-objectified love-ing, indeed, as affirming of life itself—limited though human life may be, given possible cosmic love/life.

Let me demonstrate some of the etymological (word origin) derivatives and cognates, first—exhibiting the language frolic (a kind of libido) that has led me to romp across some (often mere) acquaintance with three sorts of Greek, Latin, obviously English, German, Dutch, Hebrew and Aramaic, Chinese, Egyptian hieroglyphics, and my second language (that kind of Spanish spoken in Rocky Mountain New Mexico), as well as some French and Italian. And of course excursions into the probabilities of ProtoIndoEuropean roots so richly inflected in the several etymological resources I love to root around it, including now an Online Etymology Dictionary shepherded by Douglas Harper (www.etymonline.com).

Of course I distinguish between linguistic origins, the love of etymologists, and historical usage (a primary feature of the OED, which will in the future be available only online, not on paper)—and we can thank Derrida's followers for copping what even they might describe as perhaps-transcendental, the originary (the way I frequently need to talk about mythicity, a mythic quality that escapes all numerary-algebraic metrics).

And after those wordsmithing shafts/trenches (I owe a great deal in this regard to the ley-lines into languages laid by David L. Miller, a colleague since my graduate school days at Drew University in the mid-60s), I devote a few lines to some of the explorations of "belief" in religions, attending to some of the work of that topic assayed by another Drewid, Daniel C. Noel, in sketches for a volume that was to be entitled *The Belief Files: A Modern Myth in Media Culture*. I responded to drafts as they were aborning.

In brief compass, I move through etymological traces of love/belief, to the love/s of religion and my ongoing affection for Dan Noel, and of all the other hermeneuts and wordsmiths who witness the primary truth of Martin Heidegger's discussion of Hölderlin's phrase "dichterisch wohnet der Mensch/poetically, humans dwell" (see the collection of Heidegger's essays *Poetry, Language, Thought*). That poetry is itself a form of love—of language—is a case I hope not to have to make here.

At this point I wish I had Mac/Apple graphics/charting capabilities, but let me start from the American Heritage Dictionary definition (omitting the examples). Transitive, 1. To accept as true or real; 2. To credit with veracity; 3. To expect or suppose; think. Intransitive, 1. To have firm faith, especially religious faith; 2. To have faith, confidence, or trust; 3. To have confidence in the truth or value of something; 4. To have an opinion; think.

The etymology is Middle English bileven, from Old English belyfan, belefan, gelefan; the proposed PIE root is *leubh, To care, desire; love. Derivatives include livelong (i.e., all the livelong day); furlough (a sort of leave); belief/believe, love, libido. The outriders include especially desire, love (including lief/willing, beloved), leman/someone loved); then leave (from OE leaf/permission [pleasure, approval]; and belief [faith, German gelauben, from Germanic gelaubjan/to hold dear, esteem, trust; and then OE lufu/love (cf. quodlibet < Latin libere/to be dear/pleasing + libido/pleasure, desire).

Although I am skipping historical variations and semantics, I feel fairly confident in concluding that "belief" boils down to holding-dear, libido, love-for. But not the Christian agape (love expressed by charity toward others) nor the Greek eros (physical love). So what "I" "believe" is that I and the Other care equally for each other, and for our own selves (the pre-narcisstic libido that permits us to self-approve who we feel we are becoming, especially in relations with others/Others).

Noel's reflections begin from very literally observing some ordinary aspects of how we approach the world and others:

> These are strange days indeed for religious belief. At one time a way of spiritual knowing in the West that comprised a full-fledged faith, it has now become a narrow claim to factual truth involving fundamentalist (or New-Age) literalism, scientific constraints, media manipulation, and a pop culture in which we say "incredible" and "incredibly" every other paragraph—without actually disbelieving the usual thing we're describing.

He samples psychological and historical views of its evolutionary function, and notes how paranormal/spiritual claims are often rejected by "the general public," as driven mostly by manipulations of belief by entertainment media—and here the evidence Noel presents stretches across a wide range from *Natural Born Killers* to the *X-Files* television series (especially), and the *Matrix* trilogy.

"[T]he paranormal, the epistemological, and the millennial have been converging [. . .] and together bespeak a crisis for popular spirituality in the West [. . .] indicating an approaching 'apocalypse' of belief itself." In spite of Carl Sagan-style scientific skepticism, many postmodern academics see science itself as a fallible construction contradicting "the pseudo-scientific pretensions of all modern religion that has been influenced by the Reformation's epistemological agenda," leading indeed to the hypercredulity of the nineties, its superstitious believing" which represents "the apocalyptic culmination of five hundred years of Western religion's distorted faith, comprising a failed attempt to gain scientific legitimacy for spiritual imaginings."

"Perhaps," suggests Noel, "the [. . .] process of spiritual imagination will thereby become a more fitting faith for our twenty-first-century spirituality: not a futile pseudo-science, lost in superstition, but a valid spiritual knowing through imagining." Just such is what Noel termed an epistemythology, "the philosophical study of what we know and what constitutes knowledge, with mythology, the cultural stories that secretly shape our values and perception."

Need I suggest that the philosophical component is, etymologically, the love of wisdom? Perhaps we might revamp Hölderlin/Heidegger to read "Epistemythologically, humans dwell...," or at least that's what we love to believe.

Noel, Daniel C. *In a Wayward Mood: Selected Writings 1969-2002.* Ed. Christopher John Noel. New York: iUniverse; Part Five: *The Belief Files—A Modern Myth in Media Culture*, 2004; 189-248.

an anthology of ideas

Much of Dan's argument is developed in dialogue with these two volumes by Wilfrid Cantwell Smith: *Believing—An Historical Perspective*, 1977 [reissued 1998]; *Faith and Belief: The Difference Between Them*, 1979 [reissued 1987], and with Michael Shermer, *Why People Believe Weird Things*, 1998 [2nd ed. 2002], and Keith Thomas, *Religion and the Decline of Magic*, 1971.

Spirits

Rochelle Jewel Shapiro

My friend, Marlene, is dying. She's crippled with fibromyalgia, severe asthma, and heart trouble. The asthma medicine kicks up her heart problem, her heart medication accelerates the asthma. She rarely goes out anymore, and when she does, she has to use a cane.

Every morning for the past eighteen years, we've spoken on the phone to each other. She knows my life as well as I do. Better. She's the one who reminds me, "Oh, you'll get through this. Don't you remember when it happened before?" She gives me the time frame in which whatever it was happened and I am encouraged. And she's always behind me, praying for me and even for my other friends.

But these days, every morning her voice sounds weaker, as if her breath is being pulled through thick muslin or a straw that was crushed.

I know when she dies she won't be lost to me forever. I

believe that people live on after death somewhere in clockless time. I more than believe it. I know it. My Russian grandmother, my bubbie, was a psychic and I inherited her gift. From the time I was a small child, I'd see shadows of people moving through our apartment. Like birds in flight, they would turn and light would shine on them, and I could make out their features. There were times I could hear them, too. Even smell them.

"Daddy, there's a man in the living room who has a white beard and wears a funny black hat and an apron," I reported when I was six. "He smells like fish. His name is Yankel."

My father covered his face with his hands. "That's my uncle. In Russia, he was a fish monger. He was killed in a pogrom."

Even though I know that she won't be lost to me forever, I feel sick over the thought of not being able to call her on the phone or drive out to Suffolk County to have a cup of tea with her.

Marlene believes in spirits, too. Her grandfather Mynah often comes to her to bring news while I hear from everyone's dead on a regular basis. People call me on the phone or come to see me and I tell them things that their dead relatives are saying. I'm like a deaf person listening to them. I can't pick up all the words. I get a few and then have to guess at the rest.

"I think your mother is saying that you rubbed her feet at the hospital," I tell a client, and I know I'm right because she begins to sob.

"Your brother has taken money from the estate," I tell another client. I only heard "estate," but I saw an image of her brother wearing a bandit's mask and figured out the rest.

Sometimes I get a foreign word. "Teacherkin," I repeat, and the client tells me that her mother spoke Yiddish and her granddaughter is about to become a teacher.

Occasionally I manage to get a whole sentence. "I told you not to marry that bum, didn't I?" (The dead don't become angels just because they die.)

"Roey," Marlene says this morning, "when I cross over, I'll be around you so much that you'll be telling me, 'Will you shut up already, Marlene!'"

"No, Marlene, I'd never say that!"

"From up there," Marlene says, "I'll be able to find you a great literary agent and a publisher who will actually put money into publicizing your next book. You'll be famous and I'll be right there, clapping for you." And then she breaks into a long, rumbling cough.

I imagine her gone. I imagine sitting in my kitchen, drinking a cup of tea, and seeing her appear before me: her small body, her round head, dark hair, and big dark eyes.

"Don't you see how happy I am?" her spirit asks. "I can go to the movies with you and eat popcorn. We'll go to Macy's during Christmas and sing carols on the escalator again. We'll buy those Lotto tickets and this time we'll win big instead of the same lousy two dollars again and again. And we'll go out to eat in that Indian restaurant and we won't see the roaches."

Yes, that's how it will be, I think, and I feel so happy that I begin to cry. But then it hits me that this isn't how it will be. After she dies, her voice will be like the voices of other spirits, high-pitched and fast, as hard to understand as a scratched recording of Alvin and the Chipmunks. Even if I made us tea in my kitchen, Marlene wouldn't be able to sit down and drink it with me. Within moments, she'd disappear like the steam rising from the cup.

I wrap the phone cord tightly around my finger. On the other end of the line, Marlene is still coughing. Usually I say, "I'll call you tomorrow," but this time, reluctantly, I just say, "Goodbye."

www.miriamthemedium.com
www.rochellejewelshapiro.blogspot.com

Connections

Julie R. Butler

I used to love watching the BBC TV series, "Connections," with science historian James Burke, when it first aired back in 1978. I became fascinated with this idea of making connections between seemingly isolated and independent events. It is an exercise that is infinitely expansive, and an amazing way to gain insight into the human experience. In my journey through life, I have come to understand the power of connecting instead of dividing, finding commonalities instead of differences, building pathways instead of walls. Connecting is the antidote to divisive worldviews that separate, categorize, compartmentalize, and specialize. I know that the scientific method that utilizes such a system is effective as a method to study and learn, taming the chaos of the universe by dividing and conquering its mysteries, but I believe that it is only part of the path to true understanding. While specializing focuses energy on individual questions, furthering technology and scientific understanding, it necessitates a wider view of how the individual pieces of the puzzle all fit together if the knowledge gained is to be used wisely. This need is becoming more and more evident as humans finally come to terms with the consequences of our long disconnect with Nature.

I experienced this widening of view myself during college. I started out as an electrical engineering student, cramming for exams in computer engineering, physics, and abstract math, but never really internalizing the information. Somehow, I found my way to the philosophy department, where I felt I was learning something important about the world, even as I was discouraged from being so "impractical." I had gone from a narrow specialty to the widest field of study, where we looked at the body of human thought as a whole. That was also an exercise in making connections; I learned underlying concepts and assumptions that affect how societies construct their frameworks of understanding from within. I unconsciously continued a program of finding connections and pathways, when I hit the road with my now husband, living in our camper van and traveling to just about anywhere we could drive to—Mexico and Central America, all over the States, north to British Columbia—thus becoming intimate with the lay of the land, absorbing the energies of places, observing different cultures, and finding commonalities between people everywhere.

Then, several years ago, I began a project of trying to build my own Unified Theory of Everything, because I was distressed about the fact that the existing religious and spiritual constructs, while bringing solace to people on an individual basis, had not been successful at bringing about a world free of conflict, inequality, and disharmony with Nature. What I longed for was a new and improved way to understand the inner mysteries of the Cosmos, a new paradigm that connects linear scientific thinking with amorphous emotional experiences, so that Humanity can become whole. I began my quest by examining my worldview, at how my atheism could abide by my irrational feelings of having some kind of path I was following—a guiding angel, and an unexamined belief in a sort of karmic adjustment, where "what comes around goes around." As soon as I set my mind to these investigations, I found that my thoughts seemed to be a reflection of a larger public discussion, and began wondering if I was somehow connecting with what I called the thought-o-sphere in my journal. Then, just as my synaptic explosions were really taking off, my husband and I embarked on an epic journey unlike our previous travels, one of discovery that took us first to Switzerland, then on a road trip around the States, and then on a three-month, largely unscripted adventure to French Polynesia and Australia that awakened my muse, aligned my connections with the forces of the Cosmos, and ordered my brain patterns so that a coherent philosophy crystallized from the roiling magma of all the thoughts and ideas and emotions and feelings and memories and energies that I had been encountering on my journeys, geographical and otherwise.

In that search for consistency in my understanding of the mysteries of the Cosmos, I surprised myself by coming upon an idea for a kind of "intelligent higher power," a concept I was trying hard to reject. I could not ignore how it seems to be a universal need of human beings to connect to something larger than our individual selves or our families or even our communities of like-minded others. I came to believe this entity to be something not other than us humans, but rather the synergistic sum of all of Humanity. I believe that that which makes us human—thoughts, memories, emotions, feelings, ideas—all of those inanimate essences, still undefined by science, the great mysteries of our minds and our souls—all join together to create a whole that is greater than the sum of its parts. It is not all-powerful, nor omnipotent, but simply embodies the whole of the human experience as it continually evolves, so that we sense its presence and are awed by it. It is interwoven with the forces of Nature, its lingering energies attached to Places, unbound by Western concepts of Time, and experienced through art, music, meditation, love, the act of caring about anything other than oneself. I believe that when humans long for meaning, for comfort, for a connection with that something larger, this is what we are reaching out for. I believe that "God" is none other than People.

So instead of separating ourselves into mind, body, spirit, and emotional realms, instead of searching for guidance from above, for an explanation for why we are here, instead of continuing to separate ourselves from each other and from Nature, I believe that we need to find meaningful ways to connect everything to everything else. Connections, after all, are the very mechanisms that our fabulous brains use to make us human beings, with our thinking and imagining and dreaming and emoting and remembering, all that defines us as human, all achieved by synaptic connections. By mirroring those synaptic connections that spark our very humanness, by engaging with the flow of Humanity through creative expression, reaching out to diverse worldviews, tuning in to Nature's rhythms, and finding ways to create more sparks, I believe that we may find the spiritual fulfillment and the understanding and the compassion that we need to resolve many of the injustices, inequities, strife, and environmental problems that we all face together on a global scale.

www.julierbutler.blogspot.com

All the world's dilemmas can be addressed through the lens of the present moment. Awareness, presence, consciousness, the now. All of it! But in a world of constant clutter and distraction, how do we get there? I say: by connecting with one's creativity. This is one's access point to becoming acutely focused on the now, a timeless state of pure bliss. And this creativity is different for everyone. For me, it may be kite boarding, extreme sports, dancing, or cooking. To each's own. By accessing this presence, I become connected— connected with myself, fellow man, nature, the world around me. I become aware that we are all one. We are, in essence, the same. Just different layers of experiences. Peel those away and our pure essence emerges. By connecting with this knowledge and energy vibration, we develop a compassion for fellow man and the world around us, our environment. We understand the care AND IMPENDING URGENCY by which we approach this knowledge.

So, everyone, let's get creative!

This is a good start!

—Ryan Fix
www.pureproject.org

What Do I Believe?

Root Cuthbertson

I believe that the Earth is a precious oasis, with beautifully complex systems that have evolved over millions of years, supporting an intricate, perennial, and evanescent web of Life. Life thrives on the Earth, and over Time, various species have gone through phases of expansion and contraction.

We humans, in the 100,000 brief and early years of our development as a species, have achieved unparalleled levels of consciousness, culture, technology, and environmental impact.

We humans, as a species, are emerging from a period of adolescence into a period of adulthood.

Our human cultures and our human Choices have the power to affect the Earth.

We humans seek meaning, and the stories we tell about ourselves define who we are as individuals, families, and cultures.

The human condition is balanced between the Universal forces of fear and love, expansion and contraction, both of which are necessary and important.

During much of recorded history we humans have mostly Chosen to act out of fear. It is easier. It produces more fear. Many stories have been based on fear. During some of recorded history, we humans have ably Chosen to act out of love. It is more difficult. It produces more love. Fewer stories have been based on love.

More and more humans are Choosing to act out of love. More and more of the stories we tell about ourselves and each other are based on love.

I believe in a Divine Creator who created the Universe for a purpose. We humans cannot know the entire scope of that purpose, and we get inklings now and then.

All beings are manifestations of Divine Energy, imbued with varying degrees of consciousness. None is better or worse.

All matter vibrates with varying degrees of energy, and these vibrations resonate along various frequencies.

The Law of Attraction and the Law of Gravity describe how resonating vibrations will magnetically align.

The Power of Choice and the Power of Divine Timing describe how fate and free will amount to the same thing.

what do you believe?

There are many Universal forces conspiring to assist us, and these forces respond to the vibrations we Choose to emit.

I believe that before we are born, we human souls Choose to incarnate with a full sense of the Life before us: all its lessons, challenges, opportunities, and rewards. Upon birth, we human souls lose our full sense of the Life before us. It can take much of our Life Time to remember the reasons we Chose to incarnate.

We humans Choose to experience Time in order to assist us with learning spiritual lessons, and to experience Healing. When we humans experience physical death, our souls return from whence they came, ready to Choose another Life and its lessons, perhaps.

We human souls would experience Life much differently if we Chose not to fear death. All human souls desire what is Best, both for the individual and for the whole.

Healing is the movement of Divine Energy through stuck places. Healing requires Time.

Dancing connects us on multiple levels: horizontally through rhythm, etherically through breath, vibrationally through music. When we dance with intention, our movements serve as prayers, aligning our vibrations with Universal forces. Any group activity can focus our intentions and prayers. Dancing together uses our physical bodies to transmit vibrations into the wider world.

"We stand on the brink of a great achievement."

More and more, we humans are learning how to live in balance with each other and with the Earth. A sustainable culture is evolving, based on respect for the Earth's ecosystems, on stories that emphasize humanity's collective power, and on love. More

154

and more, we humans are learning how to dance together, how to make meaning together, and how to support what is best for each other.

www.grooveparadise.com

What I Believe

Stacey Engels

I believe that engaging in the creative process is to experience the Source directly.

I was raised in a religiously atheist household. My mother, who is now an ecofeminist activist and a very committed member of the Unitarian Church, tends to challenge this statement; she tells me we were more agnostic than atheist. I believe that's the truth for her. The truth for me was that I embraced my father's pronouncements, because he was my father, and because he pronounced them emphatically, and because I don't remember my mother challenging him. So I thought this was The Truth: religion was for the weak, and there was no particular distinction between religion and spirituality. Passive people who did not understand that everything was determined by the individual's choices, and his or her drive toward self-realization, were prone to falling back on "faith." The word "energy" was to be avoided;

it was nebulous, abstract, slippery as a snake, elusive as running water. To this day, words like "spirit" and "divine," especially capitalized, make my dad recoil. Words like "soul" and "grace" find their way into his vocabulary naturally.

We were always a bit of a strange family. We were "different" or slightly "off" in precisely the way the local minister's family might be. When my sister's and my friends' mothers made grilled cheese sandwiches, it was with Wonder Bread and Kraft slices; ours were homemade bread with aged Canadian cheddar. We watched no more than half an hour of television a day; M*A*S*H or Mary Tyler Moore or The Goodies or Monty Python's Flying Circus, very often in the company of our parents. We did not listen to rock and roll until we were older, and then it was never loudly, and in our own rooms, behind closed doors. We did our homework and chores without being asked. We had a strong sense of ethics from a very young age. There was, in our home, a reverence for art and literature and music and nature. We, the atheist psychoanalyst's kids, had a more powerful sense of the sacred than did our friends who attended church regularly.

From a very young age, I saw energy. I felt energy, and I felt when it was blocked or stagnant. And from a very young age, I exhibited an unusually retentive memory, an obsession with words and language and a drive to create that was more powerful than my very strong desire to please my parents and be a good girl.

I knew when I was four that I was going to be a writer. Again, this drive was bigger than me, because certainly at the ego level, I was not strong enough to contradict my parents' wishes that I become some kind of professional, and, if I liked, continue my writing hobby on the side. Nonetheless, by the time I was nineteen, I had dropped out of school to dedicate myself to life as a writer.

It was around this time that my life became saturated, to a truly alarming and yet exhilarating degree, with synchronicity.

My friends and I, referencing the oh-so-1984 *Repo Man*, called these coincidences "plates of shrimp," or just "plates." Though I still insisted adamantly that I was an atheist, and though I was a linear, and in many ways "rational" thinker, it became very clear that the fabric of my life was being woven by something more than my conscious choices. I began to experience life as a magical, even mystical dialogue between randomness and order—an order that was part of a greater pattern of which I could never get an "aerial view," but could glimpse in segments, or feel like Braille.

Over years, this experience of synchronicity intensified, particularly in relation to the creative process. I began to realize that it was in fact the norm that everything I needed presented itself when I needed it. That opportunity, possibility, change, and "solutions" were always available to me, and that the only question was whether I was in a receptive state or not. The universe never stops providing; I stop being open, usually when I am despairing for one reason or another.

My path as an artist has been a long and circuitous one; as well as being a quest to find expression for my own strange and magical truth in language that does it justice, it has been a study of the creative process through the lenses of the body, the breath, the emotions, memory, energy, and, increasingly, healing and spirituality. In recent years, I have been teaching writing and working as a writing coach and creativity counselor, and have never seen more clearly that the creative drive is the self's—or the soul's—means of aligning with truth and finding the state of flow. Over and over again, I have seen writers pushed to a point, through engagement with their creative projects, at which they know they must sacrifice relationships, jobs, and ways of life that are discordant with their deepest truths. Terrifying though it always is to arrive at this place and annihilate the existing version of the self, it is clear that the challenge only arises when the organism, as a whole, is strong enough and ready to remake itself.

My imagination is paltry compared to life's mystery and power. My writing "works" when I am able to get out of my own way, when I can work with creative energy and inspiration, passing it through the filter of my intellect, imagination and experience, without restricting it. I believe the interplay between inspiration and technique is, in some ways, synonymous with finding balance between faith and control. I believe that it was necessary for the individual to pull his or her power inside him- or herself, away from politics and religion, in the aftermath of the Second World War; the vision of science and reason as the beacons that would lead humanity out of the darkness we had created in the first half of the century were a critical part of the evolution of human consciousness. Yet I also believe that when the individual soul can hear itself, it knows that it is part of something great and life sustaining; something soft, gentle, fluid, endlessly generous and infinitely powerful. Something dangerous too, because when blocked and denied, It will wreak havoc until It can find Itself in harmony, because It always seeks to return to balance and flow.

www.creativebalancing.com

I believe in magic. I believe in peace on earth. I also believe that it is an infinite universe, and that anything is possible. I believe that dragons, fairies, unicorns, griffins, and mermaids, along with all magical creatures, are real! I believe that war is a horrific act that just causes suffering and death.

—Zoe Ambrosetti, age 10

Believe we are all in this together. I believe in love, marriage, hugs and kisses, holding hands, speaking the truth, asking difficult questions, feeding birds and people, and listening to children. I believe in conservation, education, compassion, inspiration, perseverance, social justice, stewardship, beauty, destiny, planting seeds, smelling flowers, birthday cakes, serendipity, and the importance of gratitude. I believe some things that are contradictory. I believe in unseen reality, the kindness of strangers, and in doing the right thing. I believe some people are stupid and others are evil, and that both should be avoided. I believe war is wrong. I believe in the power of breath, words, stories, and prayers. I believe in all the gods. I believe in myself. I believe in you.

—Ashley Carter (Zoe's mother)

I Believe That:

The universe has a plan for me. And that if I make the right choices, and think before I act, I will be lead in the right direction.

I believe that mistakes I have made are lessons I needed to learn. And that through pain comes growth. If it hurts enough, I'll change.

I believe that following my heart is always the best route—regardless of how scary that may be, and which road it takes me down.

And I believe that lots of rest, smiles, and laughter will keep me young and lead me to eternal happiness ... wherever that may be.

—Phyllis Gizzo

Faith Like No Other

Sasha Dmochowski

Falling asleep with bare skin was still too warm in the heady air that draped over that June night. The sound of my phone broke the pre-dawn hush, and moments later, my run to answer it in the kitchen ended with my body crumpled onto the tile in a sobbing heap. As the sun rose, my door opened and shut in a haze of mourning rites, a continuous parade of friends coming to vigil. Someone handed me a cigarette, even though I had quit. Nicotine addiction seemed inconsequential on the heels of the death of my best friend. With a cardiac arrest at age 22, chances are you haven't written a will, and your room is exactly as you had last left it. Sifting through Heidi's personal possessions gave me something to do each day, but I quickly discovered that this was merely a distraction, something that kept me functioning as I processed my new reality. I slept intermittently, lying awake for hours trying to navigate waves of disbelief and heartache. For some, tragedy runs right into faith; for me, grief had me running in circles.

Time warped, and my sleepless nights were alleviated with naps. One afternoon, I yelled myself awake. Seth held my hand in his, steadying the rush of consciousness that flew me back from my dream.

"I want to love you like nobody else has loved you."

I laughed—not because he was quoting Billie Holiday and not because I thought what he said was funny. It was a laugh of recognition. The thoughts my brain had formulated during my nap joined those words from his mouth, melding into one instantaneous moment of clarity.

Having grown up agnostically, and with an inexplicable confidence in Mother Nature, my existence was intuitive and organic; other than when my dog got his neck broken by a Chevrolet, untimely death had no place. I went to church no more than four times a year. For my family, the Winter Solstice was an annual excuse to feast by candlelight, the reindeer got more attention than Christ, and Easter was centered around a carefully orchestrated, multi-hour egg hunt. I had very little use for God or metaphysics or anything that had even the faintest whiff of organized religion.

At the moment I yelled myself awake from that nap I had such a strong feeling that no matter how sincere their words may be, no matter how heartfelt, no one person could love me in the way that I craved. Not God, not a man vowing to love me like no other, not even the woman from whose womb I came. There I was, lying on my couch denying a source of comfort when my world had been shattered. Why was I renouncing something that would have brought me solace? I wasn't renouncing love entirely. But the love I was offered felt so insignificant; without any personal reflection on the man himself, I craved a definition of love that inspired my faith.

what do you believe?

Given the lack of blatant spiritual practice in my upbringing, how could I define and elucidate my faith—one that had never been there to begin with? At the time, all I could ascertain was that I needed to thread into something larger, something that I could trust to sustain itself even when people who I loved left their body. I craved being woven, to be interdependent with something that would support me. In that sense, interdependence suggests disempowerment, but when being woven leads you within, it is not reprehensible to need something beyond yourself. Sometimes I need someone to call me back into my own moment, someone to remind me to stay integrated at those times when I am unable to do that for myself.

Consider for a moment the word 'enlightenment' separately from eastern religions or an association with any other particular faith. To have mental clarity and ease is literally a sense that one's mind is lightening—and while certainly I can attempt to manifest this to some extent by myself, there are aspects of my mind that I cannot access alone and singularly. Some aspects of my persona only exist by way of their reflexive nature in relation to others. How can I define or evaluate my generosity if I have no one to give to? How can I even begin to intellectually evaluate anything on a personal level if I have not already established that I exist only in relation to, and as a differentiation between Myself and Others? So in a sense, I cannot completely enlighten all aspects of myself without depending in some ways on others. But my complicated perception of myself along with that interdependence is not a shortcoming. It is a synergy of all the spiritual and emotional and intellectual interplay that makes up all communicative life on this planet. Despite their many differences, embracing the boundlessness of reality in this sense is at the heart of any of the great religious and spiritual traditions of the world.

Feeling need is just a stirring, a miniscule sip of air in the deep breath that living through a sense of deeply universal connection with other beings entails. These stirrings are glimpses of the ways in which we are all woven together in a boundless and larger entity, even though we simply cannot identify or provide explanation for it in our current modes of communication. We are creatures of exchange. We gravitate towards those who make us feel content, who concurrently share our notions of what it means to experience life as we perceive it.

But as much as we rely upon language for this connection, there is no one person who can tell you definitively where they end and you begin. Is my thought in your head? We like to think of our skin as a barrier but what is skin, other than a series of little particles, all with complete permeability? Despite our belief that we are independent and able to give selflessly, there is always an undercurrent of the expectation to receive. Attempt to remove yourself from emotional barter, and you'll quickly find that it is a fruitless endeavor. Relying on others in this way for our own self-definition, our lives are far from emotionally and intellectually linear. We do not go straight from birth to death without taking dips and turns, weaving and spun by those we encounter. If we are one swirling mass of dependant skin cells and air, and ecstasy and grief and every other emotion in between, where can we define where our interconnectedness begins and ends?

In our level of consciousness, most humans cannot see elements beyond the capabilities of our five senses. And yet sometimes events seem too coincidental not to be orchestrated. Synchronicity is an alluring concept, especially as our interdependence ties us to one another in ways that are more complex than we can calibrate. There are always forces at play beyond what we can measure or control; projecting ahead is futile, and planning anything too carefully proves inane. That second where you have exhaled all your air, before you begin to inhale, that is where breath nudges dissolution. Therein dwells the meeting of destiny and free will. What you do during your breath is of your own volition, but what lies in between is what makes the universe pre-determined.

Whatever has conspired to make us notice synchronicity (or if you prefer, fate) and however entrancing we may find this notion, when it gets right down to it, we don't enjoy contending with the idea that there is randomness in our world; whenever possible, we attempt to attach reason to all that we encounter. We like to label, to explain, to rationalize. A long history of scientific inquiry has determined that matter and energy tend to move towards equilibrium. But here's the catch: on earth, equilibrium is actually a state of randomness. The longer we study the weather patterns of Mother Nature, the less pattern we will find. Moving further towards randomness might not feel like equilibrium when it is in our human nature to order everything, and therein lies the conundrum: the randomness, the things one cannot explain: that IS the order. To have our existence be entirely random is the only thing we can be absolutely certain of, and foretell. Accepting the randomness and the certainty of change is the deepest figment of faith.

On a good day, I trust the certainty of infinite change, and I am content with acknowledging that there is no beginning or end to where I think you started or where I will end up. But some days I feel happy in my moment—so happy in fact, that I want to freeze time and never have change occur. When I take time out of the equation (if time is just a manifestation, a construct for our human convenience), I might as well take the idea of life-time out of the equation as well. Take time away from your life, and suddenly there is no floor or ceiling on your incarnation. With that existential leap, in a heartbeat, your childhood can have no relevance. And when you momentarily put aside your focus on how it was that you arrived where you are, imagine the mental clarity you can shed on your future. If we are matter on a planet that is reaching towards randomness and complexity, will we reach equilibrium? Perhaps our evolution is means to an end; the reason why we are here might be something that will only become apparent in the very distant future. Theology goes a long way towards explaining our past, but what if we had faith in our collective future? The knowledge and truths that we continuously cultivate might evolve us into a state of divinity where we become immortal. Or in keeping with the randomness of nature, a violent storm or virulent disease may quite suddenly obliterate our race.

As we have no way of knowing precisely neither where we have been nor where we are headed, how do we live in the meantime? Bowing to the notion of interdependence, how we process what we glean from others is our own personal gorgeous onus, our dance with our own destiny. A huge part of being open to the nuances of interdependence and infinite change is my acceptance of my own lack of knowing (and therefore control) of what lies ahead. To live with that acceptance is not for the faint of heart. Many nights the moon appears almost full, yet the calendar tells us that it is not quite there yet. The moment when it is perfectly round is almost imperceptible to the naked human eye. To be a little faint of heart when viewing the future, or feeling lonely or unsure of oneself translates to not feeling whole. The caveat is that the moon is always full; it is only the way in which we observe it from our vantage point on earth that causes it to appear less than full. We, too, are as luminous and full as the moon, all of the time; the vapid spaces that make us feel un-whole, or that we seek to fill, those are figments of our self-perception and therefore, integral to our nature. Embracing the illusory negative space is as much a part of being whole as is embracing the things that we deem discernable. Everything we seek is already residing within us, and only by accepting it all (even the things we cannot define, and the components which we are tempted to deny) can we be fully integrated. The more we allow the flow of interdependence, the closer we come to accepting that we ourselves are reservoirs of divinity, and can recognize our own omniscience.

Embracing personal divinity is no small feat. Ironically, the path is accessible only through the most simplistic of methods. The journey begins with something as base as resisting the urge to not already formulate a response before whomever you are listening to finishes their sentence. It is a pause that is self-contained with intent—not just to listen, but to really hear. Where that pause ends, and just before you take another breath in—that is the space we assigned to our dance between destiny and free will. How those two entities interweave in that space now has your personal responsibility attached to it. How long you retain your exhale is up to you. And how much air you allow to rush back in reflects how much sway you allow our human interdependence to hold. Deepening the pause, we disperse the urge to look beyond ourselves for spiritual guidance. For it is in the most pregnant pause that we are aware we are already gloriously full ... of our own woven selves and all that we have timelessly been given.

To fully embrace the capacity of the mind and heart requires that we also fully embrace the body—not only its capacities, but also its limitations. One thought must perish in order to unsheathe a new one. Grief gives way to joy just as that same joy eventually swirls back to regenerate once again into sorrow. Emotional cycles surround us wherever we turn, and it is experience that allows us to trust that these cycles will complete themselves satisfactorily. But can we trust that the inevitability of our emotional cycles could be also mirrored by biological cycles? Can emotional rebirth have a parallel in our flesh, and must the body then regenerate as well?

When we have no experience to rationally document a past life, to believe that life is infinite is admittedly a deep figment of faith. And yet when I fully recognize my interconnectedness with others, exactly who is the me that I think I am imagining as infinite? This conundrum becomes easier to understand when I have faith in infinite change. Anything that is acquired is eventually lost. So who I am today (my thoughts, my emotions, my daily actions) are maybe mine for my lifetime (or so is my perception) but as I share myself with so many others, and have essentially just "borrowed" these things, they eventually return

an anthology of ideas

into the infiniteness of the universe. When I look out at the ocean or up at a star lit sky it is simple for me to feel humble, and personally responsible for my thoughts and actions as I conduct my life in this body.

Equally humble when I get on an airplane, I am never without a ring that was a keepsake from my sifting through Heidi's things. It is too small for me, and I wear it on a chain around my neck. For me, taking off in an aircraft is not scary but rather, a time when I feel profoundly vulnerable. As the plane rises into the air, and I finger the ring, it is with a reflection that bears a certain personal profundity. A part of me died when Heidi did, and the faith that I have that has risen from that death is something that I cherish. I don't think I will see her again, and I don't think that she is watching over me. But when I have her ring in my hand, it triggers thoughts that take me back into myself, and make me remember the love I craved when I yelled myself awake from my nap that afternoon, so many years ago. I often feel like I know so little, and am aware of how curious I am about myself (whoever I think I am at the moment) in this body. Yet as I decipher what little I can about my current incarnation, it is with the understanding that no matter how much I learn, the learning will have only just begun. One thing I know for sure: to feel woven and to trust that everything around me is boundless and will infinitely change—embracing that notion feels like a faith I could let love me like no other.

Treasure Trove on the Streets of New York

Lynn Yang

Tonight, as I slowly walked home after a great class, in post-yoga-daze, I heard a murmur of excitement from people chatting near a huge pile of boxes and trash. I looked up and realized that two people were standing over trash bins full of books! As I came to a stop, I observed their conversation as one man continued digging in the treasure trove. It felt as if I found the pot of gold at the end of the literary rainbow. Magically delicious indeed! I peeked in and immediately started digging.

The two others were deep in conversation and barely noticed my presence. To be respectful, I did not disrupt the dialogue, but observed and listened as I tossed book over book to see what part of this cache I could bring home. This truly was one man's trash, another's treasure. From the covers of these books, they seemed to be editor's copies, bound, but possibly not completely edited and consumer ready. So many different types of books: memoirs of eclectic personalities, history of political parties, Egyptian anthropology, examination of US participation in recent wars, and even a cookbook were tossed and mixed in. What a waste, I thought, as I began to feel sorry for the authors. What if their book didn't pass the final rounds of the publishing gauntlet? What if they were to only exist in endless proofing copies? These were people's thoughts, perspectives, dreams, and possibly their only hope for economic freedom. What about recycling? I like this actually: I felt bad, but not bad enough to stop digging.

I knew that I would enjoy reading each title that landed in my "keep" pile, but I enjoyed the process of digging even more. "How very New York of us to stop and dig in the trash" was what one woman kept on saying. I didn't feel embarrassed to be part of this impromptu treasure hunt, and neither did the small group of willing participants who started milling around and joining in on the dig. I already had a good stash, and was aware that I was tired and didn't need any more books—they would be heavy to carry—but I wasn't to the bottom yet. I'm relatively small—5' 2" to be precise—and my arm span doesn't offer the greatest reach. The books were escaping me, but rather than give up or continue to stretch down and rub against the trash bin, I hopped in. Why not? It was a smarter way to do it, faster, cleaner. I began to feel a little bit of shame, but again, I knew this method was the better way to go at it.

One man offered a hand to me, possibly thinking I was stuck. I thanked him, but told him I was okay. He continued talking to me, and then I realized … well, he was a little crazy. Time to wrap it up and jump out of the trash bin. I ended up with half a dozen books, put them in one of the empty boxes and headed home. What a night—how lucky was I? As I walked, I reflected on what just happened, and what resonated with me was the continuity in the discontinuity of the incident. Each book was someone's journey, an author's voice that may have been muted or tossed away. Clearly, however, it was not waste, nor a waste because many people walked away that night with books that they will happily read while reflecting on how awesomely they scored. Also, it may have just been our destiny to meet on the mean streets of New York. The happening has inspired me, leading me to create and author this mini-essay; maybe that was their purpose?

Whatever it was, it is. It is exactly how it was supposed to be, and it happened. Possible random happening, but I have learned that nothing in life is completely random. If you open your mind to the possibility, the rest—your eyes, ears, and heart—will follow. It is time to wake up and dream! I am part of this magic, and if you choose to be open to discovery, who knows what treasures of freedom you will find?—NYC, 9.11.08

Beyond the Fields

Derek Beres

W hat I remember most are the pinkish swells on my legs—the occasional poison ivy, or poison anything unfamiliar that one acquires hiking through thick branches of forest wearing cargo shorts and a t-shirt—and the reddish scrapes that would mark the landscape of my legs and arms for weeks. Mushroom hunting: it was one of my earliest occupations, careening through the woods of East Brunswick and other towns I can't remember with Pop-Pop. He would explain which to pick and eat, which not. I never remembered; I only unsheathed my tiny army knife when he told me to incise those bulbous little critters that grew from dead tree trunks and muck.

I never ate them. To this day, I can't say I enjoy the taste of mushrooms. (Portabella are another story, but they don't grow wildly in the suburbs of Middlesex County, as far as I am aware.) I suppose Nanny cooked them the evening of our return, though

I'm not sure; the generational and cultural cuisine gaps were too wide. For example, she purposely infused fresh hamburgers with onions (another no-no), taking a hint from White Castle. Other meals included kielbasa and dishes soaked with red cabbage that represented our Hungarian-Russian heritage. I opted for grilled cheese, every time.

Back to the woods. Those weekly trips with my grandfather somehow preempted the later fascinations of my life: hiking and mushroom picking. Or, better put, mushroom buying, but that's an entirely different story and may or may not prove appropriate to this essay. So I'll stick to hiking for the time being, and plan on sticking with it as long as time continues to be.

What I remember most clearly is: dark. Those woods were thick, boy. The irony, of course, is that they were surrounded on all corners by rows and rows of carefully manicured houses, the kind that would later inspire movies like *American Beauty*, *Mallrats*, and *Garden State*, the latter two definitive examples of my New Jersey upbringing. Yet inside those woods you really were away. Sure, I was too young to foresee my urban adult life, that I would be one of those to flee the suburbs while never quite able to flee his roots. The mushrooms were secondary for both of us. For him, our travels were a chance to bond with his grandson, alongside wintertime trips to Seaside Heights to waste quarters in slot machines in order to win plastic spider rings and other useless trinkets, and almost daily walks to his favorite pub in South River, where I would try my damnedest to have my initials among the top three on the house pinball machine, downing Coca-Colas while he drank beer after beer and talked about whatever aging men talked about at two on a weekday afternoon in the early eighties. For me, they were moments away from Milltown spent quietly walking alongside my grandfather, for he was a quiet man, like his son, and like me, once, brought out of that shell mostly due to my ability to hit metal keys and watch letters appear on a screen. For some, writing is a process of withdrawal. For me, it has long been a way of reaching out.

So many of those experiences would find their way into my later life, albeit as symbols: my fascination, for one, of picking dark areas of woods to climb through. Hence, the battered and scraped skin, as I would often end up stuck in the midst of patches of sticker bushes, what Pop-Pop called spiky plants. Little could I have guessed that my first fascination with religion, which came during college—my father once told me that I didn't grow up with religion because he grew up with too much of it—was with Malory and his Arthurian knights. True, I was fascinated with images of Merlin long before, but those were pictorial; it was the mythologies that won me over. In those tales, a knight purposefully chose the darkest region of the forest to begin his quest. Choosing a path well trod would have proved frivolous. What they were searching for was an authentic experience of life, not one taken by the multitude. Little could I have guessed during those summertime hikes that that was the connective tissue amongst all world religions: the lonesome and exhilarating path of individuation, the process of become oneself by venturing where none had before—to the deepest layers of our inside world. Little would I have known that one is on a path when one does not see it under his feet.

It would be Joseph Campbell's work that opened my eyes to that connective tissue. In the human body, it's called fascia, the soft tissue threaded through our entire organism. Woven through our muscles, sinew, organs, nerves, and bones, fascia is part of the connective system that structurally keeps us intact. One time during a massage, to release tension in my shoulder, the therapist worked on the back of my knee; it worked. Reared in a culture fascinated with specialism—a doctor for every cell and bone; intellectuals who exhaust the knowledge of one particular field—what we lose in focusing on a single tree is the forest. There is great need for such thinkers, though there is a greater necessity for the understanding and integration of all parts involved in a wholistic worldview.

Granted, I'm not a "one world" proponent, nor do I seek a "theory of everything." Cultures are unique because they are independent; they are influenced, as people are influenced, by many things: cuisine, trade winds, soil conditions, climate, species, extinct and alive, and so forth. All of these help birth our political and social habits, not the other way around. How could they? We didn't create them; they were an integral part of what created us. There is (and always was) interdependence too, especially now, living in an era where trade has become such a vital component in our global lives. These conditions also gave birth to our religions. In biblical folklore, hell is hot; this image was written about and discussed in desert communities. Travel northward and thumb through Nordic mythologies, and hell becomes a cold, cold place. One is not more right simply because the proponents of one religion have printed more books and sent out more missionaries than the other. Having the most widely printed book on the planet is a matter of economics and distribution, not divine intervention. You have to read and understand (and more importantly, respect) each of the philosophies in the context of the culture in which they were created.

I've spent a lot of time in prior books criticizing Western religious practices, especially Christianity, not because of the beliefs themselves (although some of them are a bit strange), but because of how the "faithful" have translated those beliefs. I've also spent time looking at the symbolism of Christian figures in context of a broader, global philosophy[1]. Rather than retrace either of those steps, suffice it to say that what is important when reading and integrating a religious practice into your lifestyle is the understanding of symbols. Literalism has killed—literally.

----

[1] Chapter 7, *Sound Against Flame: The Process of Yoga and Atheism in America*, Outside the Box Publishing, 2008

To take things literally is to embody the ego aspect, not the transcendent calling of the philosophy. All the systems I've studied have said their share regarding ego, and the necessity of taming it. Islam, for one, means "surrender," and has to do with surrendering the individual person over to the greatness of Allah. Christianity usually actively engages in individual development (at least in how it is treated in America), yet one of the seven deadly sins is pride, which makes the entire Iraqi/Afghani war currently being waged, from a theological standpoint, a farce: you cannot use national pride as a means for religious salvation. They contradict each other. Everyone loses.

Which brings us to the greatest symbol in terms of religion: war[2]. This is a tough issue, for within my own communities—predominantly the yoga and world music industries—war is immediately viewed as something unnecessary and wicked, something to be done away with as soon as possible. From a religious or spiritual standpoint, neither of these is true. This is where we enter the dark patch of forest.

As stated, religions deal with wholism. The great spiritual doctrines—the Qur'an, the Bible, the Mahabharata—are concerned with war. Yes, I understand the modern translations by which "war" is viewed as the internal struggles a human undergoes in the process of self-realization; these theories have some credibility, though not always for the reasons they think they do. One of the biggest problems with modern thought is that we refuse to look at philosophy in terms of historical context. We translate scriptures as if they were specifically written for today. While the timeless aspect of literature is important—sustainable philosophies transcend time, and are globally applicable—we have to understand the roots of our spiritual practices. One of the (many) criticisms of the West offered by V.S. Naipaul,

----
[2] I've discussed this in *Global Beat Fusion: The History of the Future of Music*, chapter 8, Outside the Box Publishing, 2008.

this one from *The Mimic Men*: Americans cannot see past one generation. He wrote that three generations ago, and still it stands true now.

The Mahabharata is concerned with war because at that time in India, yogis were warriors—not practitioners of the sagely postures that we associate with yoga today (although meditation was most likely a key component to their practice), but real blood-drawing killers who used the principles they developed as momentum for their battles. In one of the most important doctrines of modern yoga, the Bhagavad Gita, which itself is a small sliver of the Mahabharata, the writer discusses an archer, Arjuna, being given instruction by the personified godhead, Krishna, in which the deity-made-human tells the warrior to go ahead and kill his cousins on the battlefield. His reason: duty. Yet today yogis pick and choose only certain passages from these books in the same manner as Christians, attempting to adapt the religious philosophy to their personal philosophy. We're right back to where it began: ego. Rarely do I hear discussions of Indian history, instead of the spouting of a few tenets of a few doctrines. For the most part, our treatment of Western faiths is no better. While it is true that the spiritual and historical roots of Islam and Judaism are oft discussed due to the continuing political issues in Israel—and let us give brief pause and remind ourselves that historically speaking it was the Christians who set that battle into motion with their Crusades—a number of Americans I've read or heard speak treat Christianity like the faith was born on this very land. Joseph Smith, for one, helped to paint this picture of the purebred American man and woman of Jesus.

Back to yoga: when that community denounces something—let's take war as an example—it is partaking in the same either/or mentality that Christians exhibit when denouncing, say, homosexuality. Obviously what is being discussed—the killing and plundering of nations versus someone's individual sexual preference—are dissimilar, but

what we're talking about is the staunch refusal to understand
that just maybe there is a balance, and that that balance has
nothing to do with our personal beliefs of "right" and "wrong,"
and is part of an energetic force well beyond human ethics. As
Joseph Campbell stated, "reconciliation of consciousness with
the mystery of being, not criticizing it," is the first function of
mythology.[3] If we were to offer something as a "reason" for
these things—say, population control—many would instantly be
mortified—how uncaring, how insensitive, and so forth. Then we
say things like "God" and "Divine Energy" are beyond human
understanding, and we just have to have faith. How can this
contradiction ever be justified: on one side, God is love and peace
and righteousness, and then to claim that you can't say anything
about him because he is unknowable? When did "unknowable"
stop meaning unknowable? There is little irony that one of the
most famous quotations from the Sufi poet Rumi—there is a field
beyond right and wrong, I'll meet you there—is used by the exact
community which constantly denounces things such as war, the
eating of animals, and so forth. Their annotated version: there
is a field beyond right and wrong, but we sit in the right one, so
come meet us here, or don't come at all.

So I have somewhat of a thing with logic—it does work.
Yet like science and like religion, it works in certain contexts,
and if we are attempting to put logic into the context of the
numinous, we will only frustrate ourselves. When critics state that
science can't prove that God doesn't exist, I wonder why they're
even trying to relate those topics at all. (It is usually the "faithful"
who do such, although a number of scientists engage in this
debate. I actively read all the literature on these "dialogues," and
end up vexed most every time because of the constant either/or
mentality exhibited by both sides.)

----

[3] Joseph Campbell, "Lecture I.1.1 - The Celebration of Life," Roomful of
Sky Records, 2009.

179

Let's put this debate to the test: my plumbing is broke. Let me call an ophthalmologist.

How could a scientist ever speak truly about God? Better yet, how could a priest, rabbi, or imam "talk" about the "unknowable?" Bottom line: if we have faith, we don't need faith. It's already a part of us. We can let it go.

Back to the battle. For many years I've studied numerous forms of movement: martial arts, dance, predominantly yoga. The latter felt the best for my body when I started a decade ago, so I never stopped. There is something indescribably important for my constitution about the practice of yoga. Yet during my time with various martial arts systems—capoeira, tae kwan do, a little karate—I realized that there is something exhilarating about sparring with an opponent. That too is inexplicable. When you're engaged with another human in combat, philosophies fly out the window. You cannot stop and think of the "rightness" of the fight; you don't have time. All your preparation and practice come down to instinct. You have to see where they're going to strike before they even know, and act accordingly. And sometimes, when you get hit, it doesn't even hurt (until later). There are few other times when such an absolute rush—a transcendent rush—overcomes you. You don't embody this feeling; this feeling embodies you.

It can and does happen in sport, a different kind of combat. I've played many in my life, though the one that stuck was basketball. There too moments of transcendence while on the court exist, where everything in the world fades except you and that basket. Of course teammates are crucial, but the other "side," well that's an obstacle you need to break through by any means necessary. Sure, you follow the rules, just as different martial arts have different rules—street fighting does not, but I've been fortunate to have never have gotten into any such trouble. (As one former martial arts teacher used to say, if you get into the fight in the first place, you've already lost.) Within the context of the rules, you excel, or wither. If you break a rule, it is a self-correcting practice. If there aren't any referees around to watch over the game, and you commit a foul and argue that you didn't, it'll come back to you in some manner. It always does. You don't need belief to understand this; experience alone matters.

And it is experience that matters. Belief is an abstract concept—it's a mental and linguistic idea, and does not necessarily represent reality. Anything we can conjure a word for, we can believe in. Words are concepts too; they form constructs. We construct our reality from them, like children with building blocks. Each word is a block, and as we stack, shift, and rearrange them, we create our existence. What we argue over when we debate religion is not the gods themselves (or God itself), but words. If the numinous is ineffable, if it transcends words and ideas, then any argument using language has got to be skirting around the issue. When we argue over religion, we think we're using weapons, but we really only hold plastic guns. The unfortunate thing is that the people who start the arguments too often motivate people with real guns.

Which is from where "superstitious" beliefs arose, such as not revealing your true name to another person outside of your family or clan because people who know your name have power over you, or that the words you speak could affect someone halfway across the world and that you should therefore choose with care those words you speak. This last one is crucially important in the blogosphere, where misinformation and unresearched opinion runs rampant, and you simply never know who reads what you write or how to interpret the meaning of such words; just think of the troubles misinterpretations of religious doctrines have caused entire nations. We're trapped by our own insecurities: people create realities and personalities and then offer them as "truth," and then James Frey partakes in an age-old practice—taking liberties while trying to tell a story, for the context of the story—and nearly has his intestines ripped out and fed to him on television.

One day while having dinner with friends, one woman brought up this "scandal." She was crushed that Frey's book, *A Million Little Pieces*, was not accurate to his life. She had read it, and it meant a lot to her. I asked her why, if the book influenced, motivated, or helped her through something, does the author's actual experiences really matter? A story, if told well, is bigger than the author. She became defensive. I mentioned the many books that were not "real" were still important symbolically and mythically and change lives—the Bible, for one, or take any of the doctrines thus far discussed. She was hearing none of it, because she had become so invested in the egocentric aspect of the author instead of focusing on the work alone. Stories transcend authors because they are beyond ego. When rooted in your own ego, that's difficult to understand. You only see that single tree.

There lies the brilliance of those Indian symbolists: Natraj, lord of the dance and yoga, Shiva in dancer's form. Natraj's dance destroyed the universe, and then recreated it. We have to understand what destruction means: heartbreak, stealing, murder, lying, cheating, all that and more. His dance restored balance, yet at the same time it created the imbalance. There was no first cause or fallen angels. It was always a dance, and devotees did not pray to him as Creator alone. By necessity he was Destroyer. You could plead for mercy, but you could not escape that fact.

These gods were beyond the façade of ego, because the writers who made them up understood that balance does not mean "good." It sometimes can, but sometimes it means other things. To go beyond the ego and observe the totality, that was the spiritual quest. Which makes the entire "Jesus died for your sins" idea juvenile. Not sacrifice, mind you. Sacrifice is one of the oldest mythological motifs, and Jesus was part of a long chain of men and women who partook in this ritual. Here's the thing about ego, however: a man can offer his life for others, but if the others base their actions out of the fact that someone offered their life for them, they're operating in a very egotistic manner. If one sacrifices for the sacrifice alone, ego is vanished. If one acts out of guilt associated with it or, worse, to achieve some worldly or otherworldly promises or riches because of another person's action (like going to heaven), well, they're acting out of greed. This is not the way to live a religious lifestyle, yet somehow some humans have created an entire religious platform from it.

But back to action: we define experience with words, though it is our actions that matter most. We can think the apocalypse is imminent and stockpile our basement with canned foods all we want. How do we treat our neighbors? More importantly, how do we treat the person with whom we don't agree? Do we hold their opinion to the same standards that we would hope someone holds our own, or do we simply wait for them to finish speaking so that we can talk? Two monologues in the same company do not constitute a dialogue.

By nature or nurture—the distinction is irrelevant— I'm somewhat of a pacifist. I don't purposefully fight, nor do I hope to engage in fights, nor do I like seeing them. Yet, as stated previously, I've experienced that transcendent rush when engaged with someone else in the circle of capoeira, or when defending myself in another martial art. Basketball is another example. If there was any one place I was most inclined to throw punches, it is on the court, after getting ribbed with an elbow, or, my least favorite, when someone throws a forearm into me when I jump to block a shot. I'm not blessed with girth or exceptional strength, but as someone who battles for rebounds, I have damn boney elbows and knees, and I'm sure that many an opponent has wished to express similar aggression upon me. I've come close to fists with good friends who I'd otherwise never in the world have words with. You lose a part of yourself for the game; you become something much greater than yourself, and like any nation or tribe, your territory needs defending. This is not some deep, mind-bending philosophical insight. Any man who has ever played a sport knows this, if he cared about the sport. From what I understand from my readings and watching of documentaries of war, the same holds true for soldiers. This is even accounted for in solitaire sports, like running: you turn the battle inside upon yourself. To "correct" this, to think that such a reaction needs correcting, is to subtract something essential and primal from the heart of the sport. This is no way suggests that every sport must default in a fight; rarely, do they. But to remove the rush that occurs during such moments, even if the fight never occurs, is ludicrous. The reality is you can't, for then it wouldn't be sport.

Which is why the athlete, much like the non-dual philosopher, does not seek to replace or exclude his philosophy with his reality. The totality is not only what is accepted, it's what is expected. If you live your life constantly referring to a book, or to a person who reads a book and then tells you what to believe, you're constantly living in the past, stuck in the construct of words and ideas not your own, and therefore not owning up to the experiences in front of you. Your experience has been decided and defined by another, a person who most likely is not living genuinely either. Instinct trumps rhetoric. It has to, if we are to survive.

Ego is the philosophy that we are isolated individuals congregating on a planet. The beauty of Eastern thought is that those thinkers created a philosophy in which there is one giant, living, breathing organism called the planet and that we are each aspects of it. As Alan Watts used to say, we were not born into this world, but grew out from it. Our interconnectedness and co-dependence does not imply that we are connected only to those people who do exactly as we do, behave exactly as we would expect them to based on our own lives. Wholism means whole, entire. Even the most despairing, unfortunate, and tragic aspects of the planet fall on our shoulders. If we refuse to shoulder the responsibilities of everyone, we are choosing one fragment over another, leaving us incomplete. If changing things is an inseparable part of our passion, then we must do so with our actions, not our words. The latter are important, but inconsequential to how we treat each other. If an end to war happens to be our goal, for example, we have to end all the small wars within ourselves and communities, then spread that influence outward.

I'm not sure how that would happen, though: war has been around as long as we have. There is an unconscious drive towards it, just as there is towards peace and love. Taoism expresses this beautifully: every light casts its shadow. If love is the ultimate, then the ultimate shadow is war, making them entwined. One did not create the other; they were born joined at the hip. What we need is clarity on the subject, not denouncements. Only then can we speak clearly on it.

Let me illustrate this with an important point. In the mid-'90s, I used to perform and produce shows at an arts space in Hoboken called the Liquid Lounge. There was a weekly open mic, which I often attended. One day a man, I forget his name, told a story in the form of a poem that had been haunting him for some months. He walked into his apartment building and got on the elevator. When he turned, a man had crept in through the door and was ready to attack him with a knife. There was no time to think; he immediately grappled with his assailant, turned the knife on him, and killed him right there in the elevator. He had not intended on killing the man. It was completely instinctual, and he knew as soon as he looked into his eyes that the man had set out to seriously wound if not slay him. There was no time to think; action was all he had. The transcendent had arrived.

The scene replayed in his mind, over and over. He would never consciously kill a man. He'd never wish that on anyone. Yet at that moment, the only options were to be stabbed or stab, and fortunately he was strong and dexterous enough to perform the latter. If he had stopped to contemplate scripture—thou shalt not kill—his life would have been gone. Of course such a prospect sounds absurd. Who would ever consider it? No one, which offers us insight into who we are as human beings. Our instinct is our guiding principle, our internal compass to the exterior world. It is instinct that kept us away from large animals that could eat us, plants that would kill us, rivers that would drown us. It is also instinct that helped us forge and domesticate animals that could help us, harvest plants and collect herbs to nourish us, utilize rivers that would empower and energize us.

Where is instinct in a world unapologetically focused on the past?

It's in the languaging: the prophet is returning, not there are new prophets to be heard; the original meanings of the scriptures meant, not there are new scriptures to be written, read, and discussed. I agree with Richard Dawkins's assertion that assuming the religion of your parents out of familial duty and sharing a last name is futile. It is the acceptance and partaking in the actions required by the discipline of your religion that is necessary. You cannot simply be a practitioner of that religion because you were born into it. You have to live up to its rules and ethics, every day of your life. Otherwise, the meaning behind the words of your faith is meaningless.

If your belief system calls for compassion, and you fail to show it to the people who don't agree with your beliefs, you have failed the faith. If you consider your God or gods eternally loving, then denounce the "enemies" of your religion as wicked and blasphemous, you have failed the faith. And if the scriptures of your faith were written on a battlefield and call for action in war, and you think war to be an agent of evil, well, then, you have to wonder what that says about your faith in the faith.

What it says: the writers of those scriptures were being realistic. They penned their tales by looking out their windows, not by looking thousands of years behind, or into a thought they hoped would happen instead of the world as it happened. They employed one of humanity's greatest symbols—words—to represent something larger than themselves, a process they could reflect upon but not own, that they could philosophize over but not fully comprehend. They forged the image of their times onto paper and left trails for later generations to comprehend. And that we've done, sometimes to our benefit, often to our dismay; stealing into the visions of others is voyeuristic, not realistic. Sometimes, though, it offers us important insight into who we are today, and those are the interpretations we need to discuss and integrate.

I'll close with this example from a trip to Fes, Morocco, that I took in June 2008. One of the limbs of the yoga practice is ahimsa, non-violence, which has been translated in modern times as implying vegetarianism. I have mostly lived up to that, eating fish for a dozen years after giving up all other forms of meat. (Recently, however, I also stopped eating seafood.) In some of the local yoga circles, this limb is treated as a top totem piece, often with an unforgiving vigilance against any sinner who dares not live up to it. To some, even vegetarianism is not enough, and only veganism can pave the yellow brick road to enlightenment.

Walking through the medina of Fes, a city that was, the very year I was there, celebrating its 1200th year of existence, I was met by every form of animal imaginable: fresh calf legs and heads, chickens caged and ready for defeathering and slicing, stall after stall of lamb, and so on. This was their daily cuisine, and accounted for an important percentage of their local economy. What I also felt within those tight walls of the medina was a brotherhood that I rarely feel on the streets of New York. Every eye knew every other eye, and each person looked out for the other. As a visitor, I could only gaze in; I couldn't even begin to fathom the untold secrets those walls kept. Yet the camaraderie was palpable, and while yes, I was often being sold to, there was a genuine interest in conversation (mostly about my numerous tattoos) with locals. I don't think I've ever seen a New Yorker blindly stop a tourist on the street to chat about his day.

Did I think this culture was full of ignorant heathens who were still blind consumers of the oh-so twentieth century nihilism of meat consumption? Of course not. Then why in yoga studios

187

do I hear teachers preach about the necessity of vegetarianism as an "only if" constituent of world peace? Is such an idea—world peace—really feasible? What period in our history can we point to that even came close to such a possibility? How can we today take any person who claims that their God or gods are the only one or ones to everlasting peace seriously? Can any religion take their demands and apply it to every square inch of the world, and even more unlikely, achieve success in doing so? What we need are dialogues, not only-if monologues, to see beyond the shadows of our fixation. I bring up so many questions because I know so little about this complicated and exhaustively impossible world. And yet even that last one need not be answered. Out beyond the fields there's something beyond right and wrong, and it's called common sense. I'll meet you there.

www.derekberes.com

THE NIGHTMARE & THE DREAM
Nas, Jay-Z, and the History of Conflict in African-American Culture

Dax-Devlon Ross

Outside the Box Publishing

"Rather than relying on associative leaps or pushing forth conclusions as self-evident, *The Nightmare and the Dream* painstakingly does the work, tracing connections through both history and creative analysis of the music. What emerges, or rather re-emerges, is a story of hip hop at its most compelling." - PopMatters

America is an idealistic nation. Dreams are realized here. Cultural plurality is celebrated here. Freedom is cherished here. But America is also a place where all those who seek to fulfill the promise of opportunity aren't embraced equally; where prejudice has been institutionalized, codified and thereby legitimized; where the freedoms that mark a democratic society have been stripped from far too many for there not to be an outcry of injustice. This is the contradiction of America itself- what draws us to love and loathe the nation, drives us to seek refuge either within (assimilation) or at a distance (separation) and caused us to embrace the Dream or dwell on the Nightmare.

Tracing the evolution and transformation of the dilemma through the movements, myths and moments that shaped black America and the Hip-Hop generation in the 20th century, *The Nightmare and The Dream* compellingly argues that the battle between Nas and Jay-Z at the turn of the new millennium was the latest in a long line of creative conflicts between complex, oppositional black icons. An absorbing voyage through time and rhyme, *Nightmare* situates the ideas and imagery of two of hip-hop's most intriguing, innovative and controversial icons alongside the most mythologized figures in African-American history. In doing so, this ground-breaking book explains how their truce should be read as the Hip-Hop generation's response to the tradition of conflict that has heretofore defined black creative thought. Just as previous generations have rescued their heroes from worshippers and cynics alike, *Nightmare* liberates these two artist-icons from the manacles of mindless misinterpretation by bringing some real and well-earned rigor to an analysis of their careers.

MYSTERIOUS DISTANCE

Mysterious Distance is a story of cycles: the cycle of romance, of death, of dreams ... & of corn. Updating an old Aztec agricultural mythology to suit the meaning of our times—a time of mistrust and rebellion in the ways we consume, as well as the ways we relate to one another —Beres holds up a mirror and invites us to examine our own cycles. In the end, it is a tale we can all relate to: that of love and love lost, that of life and death, and that of the mysterious distance between the romance of who we are and the life we want to live, and the life that presents itself before us. It is a reminder that as far as we run from our patterns, we cannot run from ourselves, and, more importantly, that there is no reason to: the ritual of life is a rite of celebration, even when times seem darkest.

THE LATEST BOOKS BY DEREK BERES

SOUND AGAINST FLAME
The Process of Yoga and Atheism in America

"Derek Beres is a terrific writer whose work is replete with penetrating insights and gem-like details ... Beres adds a unique perspective to our cultural mix, and *Sound Against Flame* deserves to reach a large audience."
- Daniel Pinchbeck

Sound Against Flame is an insightful and inquisitive look inside two emerging cultural ideas gripping the modern American consciousness: yoga and atheism. While seemingly opposed in numerous contexts, author/yoga instructor Derek Beres uncovers a common foundation as startling as it is revelatory to practitioners of any, or no, faith.

LaVergne, TN USA
02 March 2010
174706LV00007B/91/P